HISTORY ALIVE!

Engaging All Learners in the Diverse Classroom

Teachers' Curriculum Institute

Bert Bower

Jim Lobdell

Lee Swenson

Addison-Wesley Publishing Company

Menlo Park, California • Reading, Massachusetts • New York • Don Mills, Ontario
Wokingham, England • Amsterdam • Bonn • Paris • Milan • Madrid
Sydney • Singapore • Tokyo • Seoul • Taipei • Mexico City • San Juan

This book is published by Innovative Learning™, an imprint of Addison-Wesley's Alternative Publishing Group.

Project Editor: Mali Apple
Production/Manufacturing Director: Janet Yearian
Production/Manufacturing Coordinator: Leanne Collins
Design Manager: John F. Kelly
Cover & Text Design: Don Taka
Cover Art: D. J. Simison
Classroom Photography: Kingmond Young

The blackline masters in this publication are designed to be used with appropriate duplicating equipment to reproduce copies for classroom use. Addison-Wesley Publishing Company grants permission to classroom teachers to reproduce these masters.

Copyright © 1994 by Addison-Wesley Publishing Company, Inc.
Printed in the United States of America.

ISBN 0-201-81837-X

3 4 5 6 7 8 9 10-ML-98 97 96 95 94

Contents

Acknowledgments iv

Preface *by Joseph Onosko* v

Part I | **Introduction**
| A New Approach to Teaching History in the Diverse Classroom 3

Part II | **Six Powerful Teaching Strategies**
Chapter 1 | Strategy One: Interactive Slide Lectures 23
Chapter 2 | Strategy Two: Social Studies Skill Builders 41
Chapter 3 | Strategy Three: Experiential Exercises 57
Chapter 4 | Strategy Four: Problem-Solving Groupwork 71
Chapter 5 | Strategy Five: Response Groups 91
Chapter 6 | Strategy Six: Writing for Understanding 107

Part III | **Tools for Implementing an Active Approach to Teaching History**
Chapter 7 | Creating a Tolerant, Cooperative Classroom 127
Chapter 8 | Interactive Student Notebooks 145
Chapter 9 | Multiple-Ability Assessment 161

Notes and Credits 179

Acknowledgments

History Alive! is dedicated to the growing number of social studies teachers who have taken the risk to move beyond traditional teaching to embrace new ways of reaching their students. We, and their students, thank them for their pioneering efforts.

A sincere thank you to Mary Smathers for co-authoring Chapter 6: Writing for Understanding and Diane Hart for co-authoring Chapter 9: Multiple-Ability Assessment. Thank you also to Debra Schneider who helped with cooperative tips for middle school students and Vern Cleary who contributed invaluable ideas for student assessment. And a special thanks to Colleen Anderson and Jerome Shaw for their unwavering support and faith in us.

Our thanks also go to Pat Brill, Stewart Brewster, Michael Kane, and Mali Apple of Addison-Wesley for their expertise and belief in the project.

The staff at Teachers' Curriculum Institute deserve special recognition for their support and many contributions: Anne Maloney, Sharon Hootnick, Ingrid Faulhaber, Elona Terrill, Kelly Shafsky, Traci Cook, and Terry Coburn.

Teachers' Curriculum Institute
201 San Antonio Circle, Suite 105
Mountain View, CA 94040
1-800-497-6138

Preface

The dominant image of social studies instruction as portrayed in educational research and popular culture is not flattering. Students passively listen to teachers lecture. Students transfer facts and ideas from the textbook to worksheets. Students speak in two- and three-word phrases rather than in full sentences. Lower-order thinking and boredom are the norm; high-order thinking and student engagement the exception. Students are marched methodically through time, chapter by chapter, and must commit to memory fragmented lists of people, events, ideas, dates, and places. In-depth inquiry is obliterated by the tidal wave of mind-numbing content coverage. The past is not connected to the present. Controversy is avoided. Multiple perspectives are missing.

While the above portrait misrepresents many outstanding history teachers, it is a recurrent theme in the research on classroom practice, and it helps to explain survey data indicating that a disproportionate number of students find social studies to be their least favorite subject. Survey data also indicate that many teachers would like to conduct more active, inquiry-oriented lessons, but feel they lack sufficient understanding and training to do so. *History Alive!* authors Bert Bower, Jim Lobdell, and Lee Swenson of Teachers' Curriculum Institute (TCI) offer an exciting, hands-on remedy.

The remarkable power of the human mind suggests that instructional success may be far more dependent on generating student interest than on students' cognitive capacity, skill, or prior achievement. *History Alive!* provides social studies teachers with numerous instructional activities that can trigger and maintain student interest, participation, and, ultimately, academic achievement. In short, *History Alive!* is a handbook on how to engage students' minds.

In the opening chapter, the authors explain how the *History Alive!* instructional approach is grounded in Howard Gardner's theory of multiple intelligences, Elizabeth Cohen's work on cooperative learning, and Jerome Bruner's notion of the spiral curriculum. The remainder of the book is chock-full of powerful, practical, and clearly explained instructional ideas and methods, including chapters on how to create a tolerant, safe, and thoughtful classroom environment; how to create and conduct interactive slide presentations; how to weave in skill-building activities in such areas as mapping, categorizing, graphing, and timeline interpretation; how to create and facilitate cooperative problem-solving groupwork and orchestrate successful whole-class and small-group discussions; how to design challenging and interesting writing activities (and manage the task of correcting the products!); how to make students' notebooks an integral part of the learning process; and how to conduct assessment activities that measure what students learn.

Preface

The genesis of this book and TCI deserves mentioning. In the 1980s a number of dedicated, creative, and knowledgeable California social studies teachers began experimenting with innovative instructional approaches and conducting teacher workshops. Following their immense success, they founded TCI in 1989. TCI conducts workshops and summer institutes and has developed U.S. and world history curriculum materials for the middle and high school grades. Through *History Alive!* TCI now shares their exciting instructional ideas with a much larger audience.

I have witnessed the effectiveness of many of the practices outlined in *History Alive!*—as a researcher in the high school classroom of author Lee Swenson, as a participant in a TCI teacher workshop, as a social studies methods instructor and supervisor of interns at the University of New Hampshire, and as a staff developer and consultant working with individuals and departments in the schools. The ideas energize teachers and students alike.

Some may assert that the detailed suggestions in *History Alive!* are too prescriptive. I would disagree. Without the benefit of direct modeling in their own classes or attendance at a TCI workshop, teachers receptive to innovative instructional ideas need sufficiently detailed explanations and images of the activities they are about to attempt sight unseen.

I predict that *History Alive!* will become a giant among instructional methods texts in the field of social studies. It will be required reading in my pre-service social studies methods courses and will be strongly recommended when I work with experienced teachers and department chairs. *History Alive!* does not discuss fundamental curricular issues. It does not address the knotty philosophical problems of what the crucial goals of social education should be or what content should accompany these goals. However, once these decisions are made, *History Alive!* offers teachers a powerful delivery system. Modifying Marshall McLuhan's famous line: The instructional medium is as important as the content message in teaching and learning. I know of no better book on the medium of instruction.

Professor Joseph Onosko
Social Studies Program Coordinator
Department of Education
University of New Hampshire

PART 1

Introduction

A New Approach to Teaching History in the Diverse Classroom

History Alive! is a series of instructional practices used by social studies teachers that allows students with diverse learning styles to "experience" history. These teaching methods were developed by teachers who carefully and thoughtfully combined educational research and theory with the realities of classroom teaching. Howard Gardner's theory of multiple intelligences, Elizabeth Cohen's research on cooperative groupwork, and Jerome Bruner's notion of the spiral curriculum form the theoretical backbone for the *History Alive!* approach.

What do American students remember about the history they are taught? According to nearly every recent national study, including those of the National Council for the Social Studies, the National Assessment of Educational Progress (NAEP), and the Bradley Commission on History in Schools, the answer is, very little. A report issued by the NAEP compared 1988 results with those of prior surveys and found that the performance of seventeen-year-olds has remained stable or declined since the mid-1980s.[1] Overall, the report noted, students showed some familiarity with basic facts of history. But their knowledge tended to be uneven and failed to demonstrate an in-depth understanding of historical events and concepts.

Educational experts throughout the nation have listed a plethora of causes—from poorly funded schools to administrative inertia to a lack of parental support—to explain why Johnny has only a superficial knowledge of history. But the fundamental cause may be quite basic: Most history is taught poorly. Students neither retain nor internalize information that is conveyed in a passive, teacher-centered fashion. But classroom experience has shown that when history is taught using an active, student-centered approach, students not only remember their lessons, but truly appreciate how history affects their own lives.

This experience has prompted the creation of the *History Alive!* approach, a series of instructional practices that allows students with diverse learning styles to experience history and differs dramatically from classrooms where lecture, recitation, and seatwork predominate. Following are the lesson plans of two U.S. history teachers about to teach a unit on manifest destiny. The first teacher uses traditional teaching methods, and the second uses the *History Alive!* approach.

"A child miseducated is a child lost."
John F. Kennedy

History Alive!

■ Lesson Plan for Classroom 1: Traditional Instruction

Introductory Reading Students read pages 210 to 215 in the text and prepare a definition of manifest destiny.

Lecture Cover the Louisiana Purchase, Lewis and Clark, and the trans-Appalachian migration. Introduce how the Jacksonian era put the common person at the center of the early 1800s political process.

Movie Show a movie about the Mexican War. Students complete a worksheet about the movie.

Lecture Cover the settlement of Texas, the Texan Rebellion, the Lone Star State, the Mexican War, and the Treaty of Guadalupe Hidalgo.

Reading Assignment Students read pages 215 to 220 about the challenges facing westward pioneers and then answer the section questions.

Lecture Cover the fate of the Nez Percé as a case study of Native-American removal.

Video Show video on the Nez Percé and discuss how manifest destiny affected Native Americans.

Reading Assignment Ask students to finish the manifest destiny chapter and answer the end-of-chapter questions.

Class Discussion Discuss the role of women during this period and ask students to read the Declaration of Sentiments from the 1848 Seneca Falls convention.

Unit Test A combination of multiple-choice, short-answer, and essay questions.

■ Lesson Plan for Classroom 2: The *History Alive!* Approach

Introduce Unit Question Explain that this unit focuses on a fundamental question: How just was manifest destiny? Every activity will help each student formulate an answer to this question.

Interactive Slide Lecture Show a series of slides about manifest destiny. Ask students to step into slides and act out how Merriweather Lewis or a Native American would have reacted in various situations.

Problem Solving Groupwork Have small groups explore how politics changed during this period by viewing images and comparing music from the Federalist and Jacksonian eras.

Social Studies Skill Builder Have pairs examine photographs of Mexicano contributions to the Southwest and create a mural celebrating the various contributions.

Interactive Slide Lecture Show a series of slides depicting the Mexican War from European-American and Mexicano perspectives. Have students listen to various *corridos* about life in the Southwest after the war. Then have them write their own *corridos* about this period.

Writing for Understanding Have pairs analyze placards with pictures of geographic settings, such as the Columbian River Gorge, hypothesize how pioneers traveling along the Oregon Trail overcame those challenges, and write a list of Do's and Don'ts for pioneers.

"Learning history this way was much more than a bunch of dates and numbers. There was an understanding of history, rather than a memorization of isolated dates and names."

High School Student

Problem-Solving Groupwork Have small groups create minidramas about life in the west for a particular group—miners, Chinese, African Americans, Mormons, cowboys, women, railroad owners—and act out their minidramas in front of a slide of the historical group.

Experiential Exercise Separate students into two groups. Treat one of the groups poorly to dramatize how Native Americans might have felt during this period.

Problem-Solving Groupwork Have small groups analyze a song about the history of the Nez Percé and give a dramatic presentation of their findings complete with visuals.

Response Groups Have groups of three compare the status of women in the United States today with the aims women were fighting for at Seneca Falls as expressed in the Declaration of Sentiments.

Culminating Project Have students create a visual metaphor to represent their response to the unit's central question: How just was manifest destiny?

You can see that the *History Alive!* approach has the following characteristics:

1. Each teaching unit revolves around a central, thematic question that is introduced at the beginning of the unit and is constantly referred to in subsequent lessons.
2. Students are viewed as active learners with a wealth of thoughts, opinions, and questions waiting to be unleashed via an interactive approach.
3. Students use a variety of abilities, including linguistic, logical-mathematical, musical-rhythmic, visual-spatial, body-kinesthetic, interpersonal, and interpersonal, to experience and understand history.
4. Much of the learning occurs within the context of cooperative groups of two to five students.
5. Students assume a major responsibility for their own learning.
6. Students are assessed by how they apply the information and skills they have learned to integrated performances, not just by multiple-choice, fill-in-the-blank, or essay tests.

History Alive! Why Use It?

Since this is a comprehensive approach, many teachers have found it most effective when all parts of the program—use of a thematic question, active-learning experiences, curriculum development designed to reach a variety of learning styles, groupwork, a classroom-management system based on cooperative interaction, and alternatives to conventional testing—are used in concert. Other teachers use selected portions of the program. All teachers implementing the *History Alive!* approach, however, have taken these powerful ideas and made them their own by adapting them to their classrooms.

Regardless of how much of this approach you use, most of the strategies described in this book will require that you make some, if not many, changes in the way you teach. Why should you risk change? Here are some of the reasons teachers using the *History Alive!* approach give:

"My idea of education is to unsettle the minds of the young and inflame their intellects."
Robert Maynard Hutchins

"I have had great success reaching my limited-English-proficient students using these approaches. Slides, visual placards, and experiential exercises tap into the nonlinguistic intelligences. This allows these students to learn the historical content and then put English vocabulary to it."
Loyal Frazier,
High School Teacher

History Alive!

> *"Education is not the filling of a pail, but the lighting of a fire."*
> **William Butler Yeats**

■ **Teachers need innovative, practical alternatives to conventional history teaching.** Most teachers using *History Alive!* have discovered that conventional teaching reaches fewer and fewer students each year. They report that changes among their students—increased ethnic and linguistic diversity, shortened attention spans, lack of parental involvement, time-consuming jobs, teen pregnancy, substance abuse, and negative peer pressure—are making it increasingly difficult to teach. They need ways to reach their students that are dynamic yet practical. *History Alive!* provides an effective alternative to the traditional, teacher-centered classroom.

■ **Teachers need ways to help students see how the past is connected to the present.** Students forget much of what they learn in history classes because they have no way to apply that knowledge. Teachers need to teach historical concepts—the use and abuse of power, discrimination, democratic involvement, immigration, human settlement on the land—that affect not only the past, but students' lives today. A study of the power of the federal government to alleviate poverty during the Roosevelt administration is brought up to date by a look at government's efforts to help the homeless today. The importance of music in West African culture is brought to life as students create their own music to communicate with other class members. An important goal is to help students become lifelong learners by constantly challenging them to apply their historical knowledge to the world around them.

■ **Teachers need guidance on how to create a supportive learning environment.** A supportive learning environment can be created by urging students to take risks, praising them for their attempts, and treating mistakes and "failures" as learning opportunities. The result is more cooperative, tolerant behavior.

■ **To use their critical-thinking skills, students need to become active learners.** Students should learn history by involvement: leading, facilitating, acting, singing, discussing, drawing, making decisions, presenting, critiquing. Active tasks that require students to solve a problem, to analyze a situation, to understand a perspective, or to evaluate alternatives involve higher-order intellectual skills.

> *"Students should explore the problems and promises of living within a multiethnic environment and discuss ways in which a multiethnic society may be nurtured and improved."[2]*
> **James A. Banks,**
> **Multicultural Education Researcher**

■ **Students must be responsible for their own learning.** Challenging students to create a product (a graphic organizer in their notebook, a matrix, a poem, a written dialogue, a visual metaphor, an illustrated spectrum) or a presentation (a slide show, a panel discussion, a dramatization, an oral report) allows them to take ownership of the learning process. The result is a high level of involvement and follow-through on class activities.

■ **Students need more time to work together.** Rather than just having students work individually or sit collectively during a lecture, using strategies that depend on students interacting with their peers teaches vital social skills and leads to learning gains.

■ **Teachers who are sensitive to issues of multiculturalism need realistic ways to teach a common history from a variety of perspectives.** Teaching from a multicultural perspective, and stressing that the differences among races, nations, cultures, and various histories are at least as profound and as durable as the similarities, helps students learn to appreciate and navigate those differences in their increasingly globalized world.

■ **Teachers need to nurture their zest for teaching.** Most teachers entered the profession with a sense of purpose: to reach the unreachable student, to create a better future by educating the leaders of tomorrow, to prepare students for participation in a democratic society. The stressful reality of school life, however, has dimmed many a teacher's initial optimism. Teachers using the *History Alive!* approach often report a renewed sense of idealism as they rediscover the sense of mission and fun associated with teaching. They are reaching all of their students, not just the "best." They report that this is the way the always wanted to teach—with a sense of purpose, passion, and fun.

Learning Theory: The Three Premises Behind *History Alive!*

This approach was developed by teachers who carefully and thoughtfully combined educational research and theory with the realities of classroom teaching. Howard Gardner's theory of multiple intelligences, Elizabeth Cohen's research on cooperative groupwork, and Jerome Bruner's notion of the spiral curriculum form the theoretical backbone for the *History Alive!* approach.

■ Redefining Intelligence: The Theory of Multiple Intelligences

One of the greatest professional challenges facing teachers today is the wide range of ability levels found in the typical classroom. In an eighth-grade U.S. history class, Stephen reads at the eleventh-grade level, while Suellen struggles with a fifth-grade book; Shirley writes at a sixth-grade level, while Tricia turns out essays acceptable to a high school teacher; Juan is a skilled orator, while Dominga hardly says a word.

Many middle and high schools have confronted the challenge of teaching students who come to school with a range of academic abilities by placing them in academic tracks—college preparatory, general, special education, or vocational—as early as seventh grade. But tracking poses a fundamental dilemma: a crucial goal of history education is to prepare students for effective participation in a pluralistic society, but policies that separate students from one another according to academic ability also tend to separate them by social class, race, and language.

Academic segregation sends students at every level a clear message: equal participation and cooperation by diverse groups in society is possible in theory only. Learning theorists and psychologists, however, have recently proposed a new conception of intelligence that promises to move us beyond the outdated practice of placing students in academic tracks.

Howard Gardner, a neuropsychologist at Harvard University, argues that we must develop a new way at looking at human intelligence. "In my view, if we are to encompass adequately the realm of human cognition, it is necessary to include a far wider and more universal set of competencies than has ordinarily been considered. And it is necessary to remain open to the possibility that many—if not most—of these competencies do not lend themselves to measurement by standard verbal methods, which rely heavily on a

"To my mind, a human intellectual competence must entail a set of skills of problem solving and also entail the potential for finding or creating problems."[3]
**Howard Gardner,
Neuropsychologist,
Harvard University**

"With the establishment of a 'top track,' students and teachers alike came to assume that only students ranked at the top could achieve at the highest levels, and all involved expected less than before of those in the regular class. In this way, tracking institutionalizes the perception of intelligence as a fixed characteristic that some students have 'more' of, while others have 'less'."[4]
**Anne Wheelock,
Educational Researcher,
Massachusetts Advocacy Center**

History Alive!

blend of logical-mathematical and linguistic abilities. With such considerations in mind, I have formulated a definition of what I call an 'intelligence.' An intelligence is the ability to solve problems, or to create products, that are valued within one or more cultural settings."[5]

Gardner relies on neurological research to argue that the human mind has at least seven relatively autonomous human intellectual competencies—each with its own distinctive mode of thinking—to approach problems and create products. Below are descriptions of Gardner's seven intelligences with examples of *History Alive!* activities that tap into them.

Linguistic Intelligence

Linguistic intelligence is responsible for the production of language and all the complex possibilities that follow including poetry, humor, storytelling, grammar, metaphors, similes, abstract reasoning, symbolic thinking, impromptu speaking, verbal debate, conceptual patterning, and the written word. Linguistic intelligence is awakened by the spoken word; by reading someone's ideas or poetry; by writing one's own ideas, thoughts, or poetry; and by listening to a speech, lecture, or group discussion.

Examples

- Students write a dialogue between Patriots and Loyalists detailing the tensions between the American colonies and Great Britain.
- Students read haiku about the experiences of Japanese-Americans interned during World War II.
- Students write a eulogy to the Roman Empire that includes details of Roman accomplishments seen today.
- Students listen to oral reports on how Native Americans adapted to the land.
- Students discuss Islamic contributions to the world in the fields of medicine, engineering, and astronomy.

Logical-Mathematical Intelligence

Logical-mathematical intelligence is most often associated with what is called scientific thinking or deductive reasoning: the ability to observe and understand details as part of a general pattern. Inductive thought processes are also involved, such as the ability to make objective observations, and, from the observed data, to draw conclusions, to make judgments, and to formulate hypotheses. Logical-mathematical intelligence involves the capacity to recognize patterns, to work with abstract symbols, and to discern relationships and see connections.

Examples

- Students are given geographic data about a particular location in the United States and are told to create a city on that site.
- Students are challenged to place the date key inventions were created in Chinese history along a time line.
- Students are asked to graph and to analyze various indicators of the United States' rise to industrial prominence.

"This approach revolutionized my attitude about teaching because it showed me how to incorporate the multiple intelligences into my daily teaching repertoire."
Bill Payne,
High School Teacher

"My students love when I use slides. When they see the slide projector, they yell, 'Yeah!' Seeing the picture is stimulating and challenging. They provide students with many visual cues to help them make historical discoveries."
Mary Beth Schrepferman,
Fifth-grade Teacher

Introduction

- Students analyze a series of pie charts chronicling the changing face of immigration between the nineteenth and twentieth centuries.
- Students conduct a series of simple experiments using the deductive inquiry method pioneered by Muslim scientists during the Islamic Golden Age.

Visual-Spatial Intelligence

Visual-spatial intelligence deals with such things as the visual arts (including painting, drawing, and sculpture), navigation, map-making, and architecture, all of which involve the use of space and knowing how to get around. Games such as chess and marbles, which require the ability to visualize objects from different perspectives and angles, are also included. The key sensory base of this intelligence is the sense of sight, but the ability to form images and pictures in the mind is also involved.

Examples

- Students create a physiographic map of Latin America showing key bodies of water, rivers, mountains, flatlands, and canyons.
- Students analyze slides of paintings of the American Revolution, looking for historic detail, bias, and emotional impact.
- Students take notes using visual organizers such as flow charts, Venn diagrams, caricature, and matrices.
- Students create visual metaphors representing the relationship between the United States and the Soviet Union during the Cold War.
- Students, looking for political distortion, analyze a series of Allied and Central Power propaganda posters from World War I.

Body-Kinesthetic Intelligence

Body-kinesthetic intelligence is the ability to use the body to express emotion (as in dance and body language), to play a game (as in sports), or to create a new product (as in devising an invention). Learning by doing has long been recognized as an important part of education. Our bodies know things our minds don't and can't know in any other way. People such as actors, clowns, and mimes demonstrate the endless possibilities for using the body to know, understand, and communicate in ways that touch the human spirit.

Examples

- A group of students create a "living statue" commemorating some aspect of daily life in Constantinople.
- Students recreate life on the assembly line by drawing a small part of a picture over and over again until they feel the fatigue, stress, and boredom of factory production.
- Students stand in front of a slide showing some aspect of life on the westward frontier and act out what they think is happening.
- Students recreate the system of checks and balances in a fast-moving simulation that challenges them to check various actions

"I don't like to just sit in my seat all day. I do better when my teacher lets us move around and act things out. Those are the things I remember."
Middle School Student

History Alive!

of the legislative, judicial, and executive branches. Students sit in three groups—legislative, judicial, and executive—and must quickly garner signatures from everyone in their group if they feel another group's actions can be checked by their branch of government.
- Students play the game Scissors, Rock, Paper to simulate the development of capitalism and the Marxist critique of that system.

Musical-Rhythmic Intelligence

Musical-rhythmic intelligence includes such capacities as the recognition and use of rhythmic and tonal patterns, and sensitivity to sounds in the environment, the human voice, and musical instruments. Of all forms of intelligence identified thus far, musical-rhythmic intelligence has the greatest "consciousness altering" effect on the brain. Music calms you when you are stressed, stimulates you when you are bored, and helps you attain a steady rhythm during such tasks as typing and exercising. It has been used to inspire religious beliefs, to intensify national loyalties, and to express great loss or intense joy.

Examples

- Students listen to West African songs to understand how music is used to commemorate an event and express emotion, and then create commemorative music of their own.
- Students analyze the lyrics and music of Civil War songs to discover different perspectives held by Northerners, Southerners, and African Americans.
- Students listen and dance to the music of the 1920s to discover how and why this was a period of rebellion against Victorian mores.
- Students are introduced to the fundamentals of music by listening to medieval music and analyzing its elements.
- As students view slides of immigrants on the transatlantic voyage to the United States, they make sounds such as the creaking of a boat, the clanging of a steering mechanism, and the howling of wind and waves.

Interpersonal Intelligence

Interpersonal intelligence involves the ability to work cooperatively in a group and the ability to communicate, verbally and nonverbally, with other people. It builds on the capacity to notice contrasts in moods, temperament, motivations, and intentions among other people. Those with highly developed interpersonal intelligence can have genuine empathy for another's feelings, fears, anticipations, and beliefs. Counselors, teachers, therapists, politicians, salespeople, and religious leaders usually have strong interpersonal intelligence.

"When I incorporate music in my lessons, I reach some kids in ways that I never could otherwise. It's amazing how much history can be taught through music."
Trish Morgan,
Middle School Teacher

Examples

- Working in groups, students are given key passages from the writings of Marco Polo and Ibn-Batuta to incorporate into travel brochures designed to encourage traders to use the Silk Road between Europe and China.
- A group of students assume the perspective of some societal group—feminists, fashion models, advertising executives, university sociologists—and meet for a panel discussion with other groups about the changing image of women in the American media from the 1950s to the present.
- Students assume the roles of historical figures to recreate a 1776 town meeting to determine whether or not the colonists should declare independence.
- Students view slides about the major issues leading to the Civil War as they sit in opposing pairs—North versus South—to try to reach compromises and avoid war.
- Students work as a team to create dramatic presentations bringing to life key Cold War terms such as *totalitarianism, communism, democracy,* and *socialism*.

Intrapersonal Intelligence

Intrapersonal intelligence involves knowledge of internal aspects of the self such as feelings, the range of emotional responses, thinking processes, self-reflection, and a sense of or intuition about spiritual realities. Intrapersonal intelligence allows you to be conscious of your consciousness. Self-image and the ability to transcend the self are part of the functioning of intrapersonal intelligence.

Examples

- Students grapple with the moral issues raised by the Spanish conquest of the Aztecs by acting as jurors in a hypothetical trial of Hernán Cortés.
- Students experience the sting of discrimination during a simulation of a "separate but equal" classroom in the American south during the 1950s.
- Students examine their personal convictions of right and wrong during a recreation of the hysteria surrounding McCarthyism.
- Students create their own Student Bill of Rights as they struggle to define their individual rights in a society governed by the rule of law.
- After participating in a simulation where the teacher "loses" some of their quizzes and is unable give them credit, students empathize with the feelings of Americans who lost their entire life savings during the bank failures of the 1930s.

Let Your Students "Feel" History

Few techniques are more powerful for connecting students with the past than creating opportunities for them to step into the shoes of historical figures and react to the issues, passions, and events of the time.

History Alive!

Applying the Theory of Multiple Intelligences to the Classroom

Howard Gardner's findings that human cognition includes a far wider and more universal set of competencies than had previously been recognized offer the possibility of revolutionizing history instruction. Gardner has found that every student excels in two or three of the seven intelligences. If we accept this premise, we will begin to discover that the cognitive capabilities of our students are much richer and more varied than we had previously imagined.

No longer can we categorize some students as being "slow learners," "unintelligent," or "handicapped." According to the theory of multiple intelligences, every student is intelligent—just not in the same way. Teachers who truly believe in cognitive pluralism (the belief that every student has a legitimate intelligence or learning style that should be addressed) are well on their way to creating a classroom environment in which students possessing a variety of cognitive abilities can succeed. This leaves us with several practical questions from a history teacher's perspective.

■ **Is it possible to diagnose a student's strong intelligences?** The theory of multiple intelligences grew out of a conviction that standardized tests, with their almost exclusive stress on linguistic and logical-mathematical skills, are limited. Gardner champions a new approach to diagnosing students' strengths: observing students as they complete activities specifically designed to assess their intelligences. To assess spatial intelligence, students might complete a mechanical activity in which they take apart and reassemble a meat grinder; to assess body-kinesthetic intelligence, students might create a dance step.

Gardner's approach would take an unrealistic amount of expertise and time in most schools, public or private. An alternative is to observe students carefully over a period of time as they engage in a number of learning activities and to identify the activities at which they excel. As Gardner puts it: "My own guess is that it should be possible to gain a reasonably accurate picture of an individual's intellectual profile—be he three or thirteen—in the course of a month or so, while that individual is involved in regular classroom activities. The total time spent might be five to ten hours observing—a long time given current standards of intelligence testing, but a very short time in terms of the life of that student."[7]

In addition to observing your students, you may want to administer the multiple-intelligence test "Where Does Your Intelligence Lie?" on page 13. This initial measure will give you a snapshot view of each student's cognitive strengths and, combined with careful observation, will create accurate intelligence profiles.

■ **Should instruction be individually designed to tap into each student's cognitive strength?** After diagnosing each student for his or her cognitive strengths, Gardner advocates that the instructor create a curricular program to meet the needs of that individual learner. In an ideal world this would be wonderful, but in the real world, it is impractical. Rather than creating individualized lessons focused on each student's cognitive strengths, create lessons in which each history objective is taught via as many of the different intelligences as possible so that all students can have access to the curricular

---

"According to a survey from the National Institute for Development and Administration at the University of Texas, we remember only 10 percent of what we read, 20 percent of what we hear, 30 percent of what we see, 50 percent of what we see and hear, and 90 percent of what we do and say."[6]

Danielle Lapp,
Memory Researcher

Students use an array of intelligences to prepare and present their interpretation of Fred Small's song "Heart of the Appaloosa," which chronicles the displacement of the Nez Percé.

Where Does Your Intelligence Lie?

This quiz will help you identify your areas of strongest intelligence. Read each statement. If it expresses some characteristic of yours and sounds true for the most part, jot down a T. If it doesn't, mark an F. If the statement is sometimes true and sometimes false, leave it blank.

1. _____ I'd rather draw a map than give someone verbal directions.
2. _____ If I am angry or happy, I usually know why.
3. _____ I can play (or used to play) a musical instrument.
4. _____ I can associate music with my moods.
5. _____ I can add or multiply quickly in my head.
6. _____ I can help a friend sort out strong feelings because I successfully dealt with similar feelings myself.
7. _____ I like to work with calculators and computers.
8. _____ I pick up new dance steps fast.
9. _____ It's easy for me to say what I think in an argument or debate.
10. _____ I enjoy a good lecture, speech, or sermon.
11. _____ I always know north from south no matter where I am.
12. _____ I like to gather together groups of people for parties or special events.
13. _____ Life seems empty without music.
14. _____ I always understand the drawings that come with new gadgets or appliances.
15. _____ I like to work puzzles and play games.
16. _____ Learning to ride a bike (or skate) was easy.
17. _____ I am irritated when I hear an argument or statement that sounds illogical.
18. _____ I can convince other people to follow my plans.
19. _____ My sense of balance and coordination is good.
20. _____ I often see patterns and relationships between numbers faster and easier than others.
21. _____ I enjoy building models (or sculpting).
22. _____ I'm good at finding the fine points of word meanings.
23. _____ I can look at an object one way and see it turned sideways or backwards just as easily.
24. _____ I often connect a piece of music with some event in my life.
25. _____ I like to work with numbers and figures.
26. _____ I like to sit quietly and reflect on my inner feelings.
27. _____ Just looking at shapes of buildings and structures is pleasurable to me.
28. _____ I like to hum, whistle, and sing in the shower or when I'm alone.
29. _____ I'm good at athletics.
30. _____ I enjoy writing detailed letters to friends.
31. _____ I'm usually aware of the expression on my face.
32. _____ I'm sensitive to the expressions on other people's faces.
33. _____ I stay "in touch" with my moods. I have no trouble identifying them.
34. _____ I am sensitive to the moods of others.
35. _____ I have a good sense of what others think of me.

© Addison-Wesley Publishing Company, Inc.

History Alive!

content and develop the full range of their intellectual abilities. Consider how the following two lessons tap into most, if not all, of Gardner's seven intelligences.

Example 1. Students explore the concept of manifest destiny as seen through Native-American eyes by analyzing a song about the displacement of the Nez Percé during the late 1800s. After listening to the song (musical), students are assigned to groups of four (interpersonal) and are given the lyrics and resource documents (linguistic) on one of nine verses from Fred Small's song "Heart of the Appaloosa." Groups interpret their lyrics (logical-mathematical) and make a presentation of their analysis—with the help of slides of the Nez Percé (visual-spatial), a visual representation of the verse (visual-spatial), and their own creativity (intrapersonal). A discussion (interpersonal) on Native-American displacement follows. Then students read (linguistic) a letter to the "Great Chief in Washington" from Chief Seattle about the plight of Native Americans at the turn of the century. They respond to the letter by writing a statement (linguistic) about their own feelings (intrapersonal) on Native-American displacement.

This lesson uses six of the seven intelligences. Although the seventh intelligence (body-kinesthetic) was not overtly addressed, it is used briefly when students give their class presentations.

Example 2. Students get an overview of Mexican history—from the conquest of the Aztecs to the 1910 Mexican Revolution—by examining a series of murals depicting four hundred years of the nation's history. Students sit in groups (interpersonal) to identify the symbols (visual-spatial) in a number of Mexican murals. They are then challenged to place the murals into three groups corresponding to the three artists they think painted them (logical-mathematical). This is followed by a class discussion (linguistic) about the style, themes, and techniques used in each mural. Then students place the murals in chronological order according to the history of Mexico (logical-mathematical). Next, they see a slide of each mural (visual-spatial) and are asked to act out what they think is happening (body-kinesthetic) and then to interpret how the mural affects them personally (intrapersonal). Finally, students create a mural of their own (visual-spatial) with an accompanying written description (linguistic).

The unused intelligence (musical-rhythmic) might easily accompany this lesson in the form of Mexican background music.

■ **Is it important to challenge students to use intelligences other than their dominant ones?** Some teachers initially resist using the *History Alive!* approach because they fear the use of the multiple intelligences in their classroom would be inappropriate. For example, teachers of learning-disabled, English-as-a-second-language, and "lower-track" students occasionally worry that an approach using the multiple intelligences still relies too heavily on linguistic intelligence; advanced-placement and honors teachers sometimes feel that asking their students to make music or to draw during history class would waste time.

All students can benefit from a curriculum that includes the multiple intelligences. Students who are not strong linguistically should have access to historical concepts through other intelligences, say musical-rhythmic or

---

"This approach draws kids into history because the strategies are crafted with special attention to all intelligences."

**Yvette Sarnowski,
High School Teacher and
Curriculum Coordinator**

Cognitive Pluralism: More Than Buzzwords

Every social studies objective should be taught through as many of the intelligences as possible. This allows for more equitable learning by giving all students access to ideas.

Introduction

body-kinesthetic, but they also should be challenged linguistically. In fact, these students are better able to perform linguistically because they truly understand the concepts they learn via their strong intelligences. Likewise, highly skilled linguistic students—who predominate advanced-placement and honors classes—should be challenged to improve nonlinguistic intelligences. They should be given a chance to improve their interpersonal skills by working with fellow students, to use their intrapersonal intelligence to feel empathy for others, and to listen to music that may inspire them. Teachers need to see themselves not only as instructors of history, but as cultivators of intelligence.

The challenge for the history teacher is to create lessons that simply and elegantly tap into as many of the seven intelligences as possible, while at the same time teach the required history content. In fact, since history is the record of all types of human achievement, what better way to teach it than in a curriculum rich in a variety of forms of human expression? In later chapters, you will discover how to weave the multiple intelligences into every lesson you develop.

■ Cooperative Interaction: A Vital Key to Learning

The second theoretical premise behind the *History Alive!* approach is easily stated: cooperative interaction leads to learning gains. Researchers report that cooperative groupwork promotes higher student achievement and productivity than either competitive or individualistic teaching methods; the more students have the opportunity to interact with each other—by discussing a controversial topic, preparing one another for a quiz, interviewing each other—the more they will learn and remember.

However, sociologists have discovered when students perform a collective task, some are more influential than others. Elizabeth Cohen has found that students expect certain performances from one another.[9] Students prejudge what their peers will be able to contribute on the basis of perceived academic ability and peer status. As a group, they believe some students are "low status" and others are "high status." When high-status and low-status students work together, a self-fulfilling prophecy results: perceived high-status students tend to interpret most of the questions, talk more, and have their opinions accepted more than perceived low-status students. This unequal pattern of interaction results in unequal learning gains: high-status students, because they interact more, learn more; low-status students, because their interaction is severely limited, learn less.

Virtually every teacher faces the problem of unequal status interaction. Researchers have shown that an unequal status order exists in every classroom, no matter how homogeneous a classroom may appear.[10] Unless we acknowledge this problem and deal with it frankly, our efforts at increasing student interaction may ultimately make things worse if high-status students reap all the benefits.

Fortunately, research has uncovered practical ways to combat the problem. Cohen has found that if teachers use heterogeneous groups and learn how to change expectations for competence, low-status students participate more and high-status students do not dominate. Cohen's work has focused exclusively on students working in groups of four or five, and it is discussed in greater detail in Chapter 4.

"Groupwork is an effective technique for achieving certain kinds of intellectual and social learning goals. It is a superior technique for conceptual learning, for creative problem solving, and for increasing oral language proficiency."[8]

Elizabeth Cohen,
Professor of Education,
Stanford University

Cooperative Learning: Not Just for Small Groups

Cooperative learning is more than just a strategy for groupwork. It is the establishment of a nurturing environment that helps students learn in whole-class settings as well.

History Alive!

Many of the techniques Cohen has found effective with small groups can be used with larger groups and paired instruction as well. Using these ideas in combination with Howard Gardner's theory of multiple intelligences, you can create effective cooperative interaction. All students in the heterogeneous classroom become convinced they have a valued skill to contribute. Much of this book will show you how to create your own lessons designed to combat the problem of unequal status interaction by tapping into the multiple intelligences—enabling you to create cooperative interaction that leads to learning gains for *all* of our students.

■ All Students Can Learn: The Spiral Curriculum in Action

The third theoretical premise behind the *History Alive!* approach is the idea of the spiral curriculum. Championed by educational theorist Jerome Bruner in his landmark book *The Process of Education,* this is the belief that all students can learn if a teacher shows them how to think and discover knowledge for themselves. "The quest," according to Bruner, "is to devise materials that will challenge the superior student while not destroying the confidence and will-to-learn of those who are less fortunate." You can apply the concept of the spiral curriculum at both the activity and the unit level.

The Spiral Curriculum at the Activity Level

Carefully structure each lesson to lead your students through a step-by-step process of self-discovery. Students should first explore a historic event, idea, or personality by using elemental cognitive skills—observation, description, identification, recall—and then spiral to ever-higher levels of cognition such as synthesis, application, and interpretation. This enables students from a variety of academic levels to learn together effectively and gives all students the cognitive building blocks they need to reach what Fred Newmann and Joseph Onosko call higher-order thinking.[12]

Defined broadly, higher-order thinking is the challenged and expanded use of the mind; lower-order thinking is the routine, mechanistic application of the mind.[13] Lower-order and higher-order thinking skills can be carefully dovetailed into one another to form a seamless series of steps that challenges students to learn more by progressing from the fundamental to the sophisticated.

An activity on late-nineteenth-century attitudes towards immigrants arriving in the United States illustrates how to use the spiral curriculum at the activity level. The teacher begins the activity by showing a slide of a political cartoon depicting the arrival of a Southern European immigrant in New York. The immigrant is greeted by five scornful men, all established American residents, whose body language suggests they have little tolerance for this new wave of immigrants. Behind each resident looms the shadow of his own poor immigrant past. The teacher begins by asking questions that build toward higher-order thinking skills: What do you see here? What does the immigrant look like? Describe the reaction of the residents greeting the immigrant. How will the immigrant react? What is looming behind these men? Were the residents once immigrants themselves? If so, why are they rejecting the new arrival? Is the cartoonist pro-immigrant or anti-immigrant? What is ironic about this cartoon? Do you see any parallels between this

---

"Any subject can be taught effectively in some intellectually honest form to any child at any stage of development. Through a spiral curriculum students learn progressively more difficult concepts through step-by-step self-discovery."[11]

Jerome Bruner,
Educational Theorist

"Teachers appreciate the depth of historical exploration that the spiral curriculum creates. Within a single activity, students are introduced to the basics of a topic, then quickly immerse themselves in the history through dramatizations, simulations, and the like—exercises that require them to use higher-order thinking skills. By the end of an activity, they really understand the complexities of the history because they have, in a sense, lived it."

Pete Pitard,
San Diego County Social Studies Coordinator

Introduction

By carefully spiraling your questions from the basic to the complex, you can give your students the building blocks they need to use higher-order thinking skills to derive meaning from political cartoons.

cartoon and immigration today? By carefully spiraling questions from the fundamental to the sophisticated, the teacher helps students interpret the cartoon.

The teacher's next set of questions are: What is a political cartoon? What are the devices a cartoonist uses to get across a message? Why do we have political cartoons? Students extend their learning beyond the single cartoon by generalizing about the purpose of political cartoons. They learn how the cartoonist uses symbolism, irony, caricature, exaggeration, slogans, color, and stereotypes to convey a message.

Next, students analyze several other cartoons that depict differing attitudes toward immigration at the turn of the century through a step-by-step process that spirals from the basic to the complex. They make a quick sketch of each cartoon, list the symbols they find, and describe the cartoon by identifying the characters and their actions. Finally, they discuss what message they think the cartoonist is trying to convey. When students have finished this process of self-discovery, they are ready to synthesize what they have learned. The teacher challenges them to place the cartoons along a political spectrum—from tolerant to intolerant—and to discuss the variety of perspectives Americans held about immigration during the turn of the century. They then make connections between past and present attitudes.

Had the teacher begun this lesson by showing the political cartoon of the arriving immigrant and asking: What is ironic about the xenophobic reaction of the established residents to the arriving immigrants? few, if any, students would have had much to say. Instead, students were asked to describe what they saw, draw a sketch, and discuss basic questions before they were challenged to use higher-order thinking skills such as analysis, interpretation, and synthesis. This gave all students, regardless of academic background, the

Benjamin Bloom's Taxonomy[14]: A Guide for Creating Questions

Knowledge The ability to recall specifics, universals, methods, processes, and patterns

Comprehension The ability to translate, interpret, and extrapolate

Application The ability to use abstractions in concrete situations

Analysis The ability to analyze elements, relationships, and organizational principles

Synthesis The ability to put together elements and parts to form a whole

Evaluation The ability to make judgments about the value of ideas, works, solutions, and methods

---

"Using the spiral curriculum allows students to apply concepts they learned earlier to help them solve high-level problems. For example, students use their knowledge of the physiographic features of the United States—which they learned at the beginning of the unit—to help them figure out how different Native American groups adapted to the land."
Nancy Byrne,
Middle School Teacher

History Alive!

necessary building blocks to move toward higher-order thinking. This is the genius of the spiral curriculum in an individual activity.

The Spiral Curriculum at the Unit Level

Just as each activity can be structured with the spiral curriculum in mind, so too can each teaching unit. This is accomplished by building every unit around a thematic question. A unit on the Great Depression and the New Deal, for example, might center around a question such as: Should the federal government give more assistance to the needy? A unit on imperialism in Africa might challenge students to answer this question: Are the Europeans to be praised for their colonial actions in Africa? The activities in the unit spiral from the basic to the complex, encouraging students to consider the central question using ever-more-sophisticated thinking skills. The final activity is a culminating project that challenges students to synthesize and apply their historical knowledge.

The spiral curriculum can be seen in action in a unit about manifest destiny. The unit's central question is: How just was manifest destiny? In the first section of the unit students might consider the central question by viewing slides illustrating manifest destiny. As they discuss and analyze them, they learn the basics about the Louisiana Purchase, the travels of Lewis and Clark, and the trans-Appalachian migrations. Then they consider manifest destiny from William Clark's point of view as they examine original journal entries and drawings. They use this information to create their own account of life on the new frontier. This gives students a basic understanding of manifest destiny as seen from one perspective. In subsequent sections, they are challenged to use higher-order thinking skills to consider manifest destiny from a variety of perspectives.

In the next section students examine images representing Mexicano contributions to Southwest culture such as ranching, irrigation, and architecture. This provides them with another perspective to keep in mind when they study the Lone Star Revolt and the Mexican War. Students apply their new knowledge to analyze a *corrido,* or Mexican folk song, and then create a *corrido* of their own to explain manifest destiny from a Mexicano perspective.

Next, students view manifest destiny from the settlers' perspective. First, they see photographs of geographic challenges facing the westward pioneers and hypothesize how the settlers overcame them. They then apply their new knowledge to create a list of Do's and Don'ts for pioneers. A final activity encourages them to create minidramas depicting how a wide range of pioneers—Mormons, forty-niners, frontier women, Chinese Americans, the Donner party, railroad owners, African Americans, cowboys—lived in the new lands they settled. All students are able to participate because, through the series of spiraling steps, they gained a common knowledge base.

In the final section of the unit students analyze manifest destiny from a Native-American perspective. The section begins with an experiential activity in which one group of students feels the despair of having their "land" taken from them as their desks are seized by another group who are "destined" to have that prime space. This activity gives most students a new perspective with which to analyze slides chronicling Native-American removal. Students act out the scenes in many of the slides to gain a Native-American perspective on westward expansion. Then students form groups to analyze

Introduction

Students examine historical images of Mexicano contributions to Southwest culture, such as this one showing strong family unity.

"I thought I was incapable of learning history. Before it was just a textbook, lectures, and a bunch of jumbled facts. But the way this class was organized made sense. It really made history clear."
High School Student

stanzas of a song chronicling the retreat of the Nez Percé from the U.S. Cavalry and to present dramatic accounts of the historic retreat. Finally, students read a letter written by Chief Seattle of the Suwamish tribe to President Pierce in 1855 regarding the purchase of Suwamish land and write a presidential speech responding to Chief Seattle's concerns. Notice how all of these activities spiral: students have a basic human experience, which they connect to the past; they learn about Native-American removal in general; they explore a detailed case study of one group of Native Americans; and they apply all that they learned in a sophisticated writing activity.

This unit culminates with a project challenging students to use higher-order thinking skills to synthesize and apply what they have learned. Groups create visual metaphors representing manifest destiny as seen through the eyes of four people: an early explorer, a Mexicano, a settler, and a Native American. The metaphors indicate students' final stand on the central question: How just was manifest destiny?

By leading students through a step-by-step process of self-discovery, you insure that students from a variety of academic levels will have the conceptual information they need to answer complex questions. Design each lesson with the spiral curriculum in mind: each unit should incorporate activities that dovetail into one another, challenging students to use higher-order thinking skills. Units that incorporate this feature will be highly effective in the heterogeneous classroom and will lead all students to a greater understanding and appreciation of history.

> "Theory. Theory. Theory. Teachers always hear theories. But the beauty of this approach is that finally theory is put into practice. This changes what happens in the classroom."
>
> **Loyal Frazier,**
> **High School Teacher**

Putting Theory into Practice

The rest of this book is devoted to a detailed discussion of how you can put the three theoretical premises behind the *History Alive!* approach—the theory of multiple intelligences, the focus on cooperative interaction, and the idea of the spiral curriculum—into practice in your classroom.

The first six chapters show how you can apply six powerful teaching strategies—Interactive Slide Lectures, Social Studies Skill Builders, Experiential Exercises, Problem-Solving Groupwork, Response Groups, and Writing for Understanding—to your own classroom. Chapter 7 gives a step-by-step approach you can use to create a cooperative, tolerant classroom environment, the key to experiencing success with all *History Alive!* teaching strategies. Chapter 8 describes how Interactive Student Notebooks will help students organize and process what happens in class. And finally, Chapter 9 gives you practical advice on innovative ways to assess your students.

PART 2

Six Powerful Teaching Strategies

CHAPTER 1

Strategy One: Interactive Slide Lectures

This strategy turns what is usually a passive, teacher-centered activity —lecturing—into a dynamic, participative experience. Students view, touch, interpret, and act out historic images that are projected onto a large screen in front of the classroom. As the discussion unfolds, the teacher writes notes on an overhead transparency that is projected on a second, smaller screen in a front corner. Students simultaneously see an image and notes, helping them to learn and remember salient ideas that most students soon forget after the traditional lecture.

Kelly Shafsky remembers the first time he taught about turn-of-the-century European immigration to his high school students. "I might as well have been lecturing about economic history in the 1500s," he laments. Despite a well-organized outline and interesting personal anecdotes—his great-great-grandfather was one of thousands of European Jews fleeing the Czar's army in the 1890s—his students asked few questions and left class "completely unmoved and seemingly unconcerned" about the great wave of European immigration.

Kelly was puzzled and even angry at his students' lack of response. After reflecting on the lesson, he decided it wasn't him or the topic that was to blame for his students' apathy, but the teaching mode.

The next year Kelly prepared a different type of lesson on immigration. First, he made a slide of one powerful photograph to illustrate each of ten main points he wanted to make. On the day of the lesson, he changed his students' seating arrangement so that each student could see the projected slide and the overhead projection, leaving space in front for students to touch the slide screen. He began the lesson with an image of immigrants waving goodbye to their loved ones from a crowded dock in Europe.

"I'll never give a regular lecture again."

Kelly Shafsky

"Analyzing visual images helps me learn history because I have to put myself in the picture and think as if I were there."

High School Student

"I can learn a lot better when the teacher uses slides in his lectures. It is like he is writing a whole book in my mind."

High School Student

History Alive!

"That first slide was like magic," Kelly says. "I asked students to describe everything they saw in the picture and then to step into the slide and act out what they thought was happening." Kelly pretended to have a microphone in his hand as he interviewed his students: Why are you leaving? What do you hope to gain in America? How do you feel about this? With the slide as a prop and the semi-dark room for cover, Kelly's students were soon able to answer his questions in great detail and with appropriate humor.

When the five-minute role-play was over, Kelly asked students for reasons immigrants left Europe. Several hands shot up and soon Kelly was immersed in a rich discussion. He listed more than fifteen substantive reasons for immigration on the overhead projector—most of them supplied by the students.

Kelly continued to use slides in this interactive way for the rest of the lesson. When he showed a slide of the steerage deck, he placed students "on the deck" in front of the slide and moved the projector back and forth like a rocking ship; when he showed the main hall at Ellis Island, he sat students on chairs in front of the slide, gave them notes to attach to themselves to represent how immigrants were tagged by nationality, and acted like an immigration officer, Anglicizing their names as they were processed. Students were eager to act out what they thought the immigrants would be doing and saying.

Powerful historical photographs, such as this one showing a group of European immigrants huddled aboard a ship at the turn of the century, can be used to actively engage visual learners in a host of creative and exciting ways.

By the end of the lesson, Kelly's students were motivated to learn more about immigration and to read a short play he had written about his own family's immigration history. They even shared their own family's stories. "I was amazed at how differently students reacted to this lesson compared to my lesson the year before. If you give students a chance to think for themselves and to go back in time to relive a bit of history, you create a much more powerful learning experience."

Moving Beyond the Traditional Lecture

Educational historian Larry Cuban notes that little structural change has occurred in classroom teaching in the last one hundred years of public schooling. The majority of classroom time is spent on teachers lecturing, students listening, students reading textbooks, and students filling out worksheets.[1] Most social studies teachers teach history in the same way they learned it: using the lecture and discussion approach. Traditional lectures, however, are increasingly falling on deaf ears. Many students simply cannot learn from lectures, no matter how amusing or storylike.

Students who are not strong linguistic learners do not process information they hear in lectures. Often only the linguistically gifted students answer questions during class discussion, giving the majority of students little opportunity for interaction. Teachers who lecture day after day often find their job monotonous and tiring. The fun of teaching becomes an ideal of the past as they constantly contend with restless classes and classroom crises. Even if teachers deliver eloquent lectures that manage to retain student interest, many students seem to remember little of the history they heard when it comes time for the exam.

The *History Alive!* method does not give up on lecturing altogether. Rather, it advocates a more effective way to lecture that encourages more interaction by tapping into students' broader range of intelligences. This chapter describes how you can use slides in a truly interactive way to illustrate the historical points you want to make. This will give you several advantages:

- Slides capture student interest and give you something to talk about and rely on as an effective prop.
- You no longer need to be the center of attention, because you will be sharing the spotlight with an image from the past.
- Historical images serve as strong visual mnemonics that help many
  students remember historical concepts.
- Students with strong visual ability perform better on linguistic tasks after having "seen" the information.
- Students become skilled at pointing out details of historical images.
- You will learn and have new insights along with your students.
- Showing slides is an effective way to review the previous day's lecture.

> "This technique is a great strategy. It can help kids all over the world. I feel this way because you can actually see the history happen. When you just have to read it out of a textbook it makes you want to say: 'Teacher, can I go to the bathroom?' And then stay there until recess."
> **Middle School Student**

> "My students really enjoy Interactive Slide Lectures. They like the structure that note-taking provides, but they also like being able to be participative and spontaneous."
> **Trish Morgan, Middle School Teacher**

History Alive!

Setting up Your Classroom

Careful attention to your classroom's "geography" is essential for a successful Interactive Slide Lecture. Most classroom arrangements inhibit interaction; students often sit in long rows where the "lucky ones" get the last seats and occasional naps. The front of many classrooms is a clutter of desks, tables, and file cabinets that, in effect, barricade the teacher from the students.

The basic classroom configuration for an Interactive Slide Lecture is parliamentary style, with two groups of desks facing each other. Leave ten feet or more between the groups—enough space to discourage casual conversation, but close enough to allow students on one side to hear students on the other. The center aisle allows students to walk to the front of the classroom quickly and gives you room to project a slide on a wide screen without getting heads in the projection. Leave a staging area in the front of the classroom for students to interact with the images. Project the slide onto a large screen and the overhead projection on a smaller screen in a front corner or on the front wall, allowing students to view the image and take notes at the same time. This technique gives students who are slower at taking notes time to write without you turning off the overhead projector to the inevitable chorus of, "We're not finished yet!"

Most classrooms are simply too small to fit thirty-six to forty active adolescents, but the layout of your room is essential to giving a successful Interactive Slide Lecture. Here are tips teachers have found helpful in creating a classroom layout that works:

- The first time you arrange your classroom for an Interactive Slide Lecture, choose a time when students are not in class and you can play with different configurations. Create a plan that works well with your classroom; it doesn't need to look exactly like the one shown opposite.
- Use the largest slide projection screen you can, preferably 72 by 72 inches. If you can't afford to buy such a large screen, make one. Remove the chalk rail on your front chalkboard and tape swatches of butcher paper to the wall, covering floor to ceiling at a width of about 72 inches.
- Use a small screen for the overhead projection. Hang your small projector screen from the ceiling in one of the front corners of your classroom, angling it towards the desks. You can also use butcher paper or a white wall. You will want to keep the overhead projection on throughout the lecture without throwing a lot of light on the slide screen.
- Use a zoom lens on your slide projector to make your images as large as possible. Most carousel projectors come with a standard 127-mm lens, which, in most classrooms, will not project a large enough image. A 102- to 152-mm zoom lens will. But before you run down to the photo store, measure the distance between the slide projector and the screen and be ready to tell the salesperson that distance and that you would like to project an image at least 72 inches wide.

Big Screens, Cheap

The larger the projected image, the more the student interaction. You can make a large screen by taping together two 4-foot-by-8-foot, 1-inch-thick insulating foam boards, found in most building-supply stores.

Chapter 1

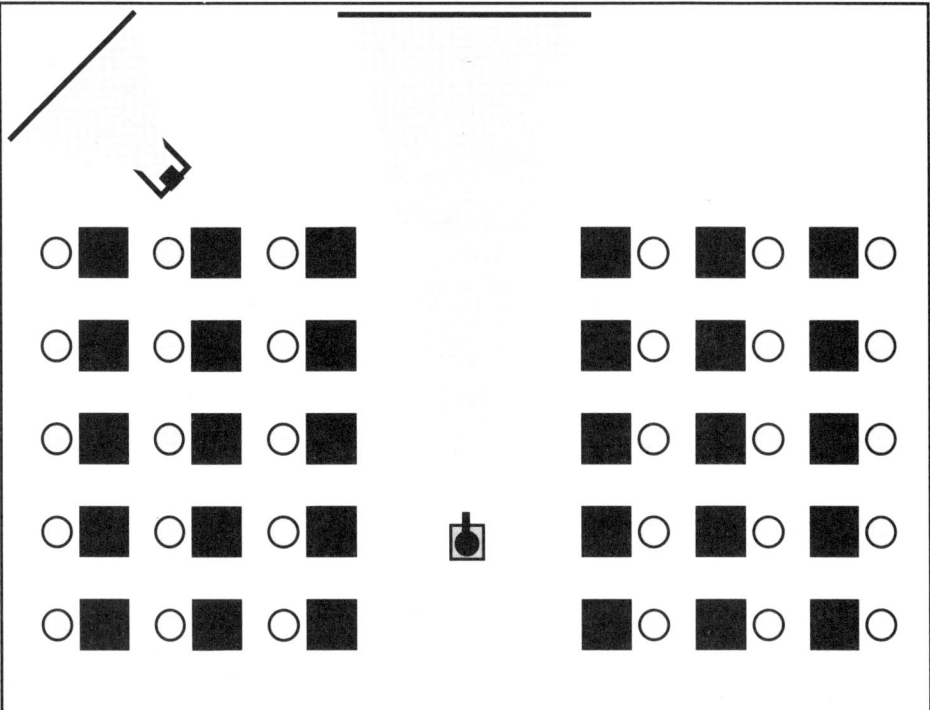

This is the most common classroom arrangement for Interactive Slide Lectures, with a wide center aisle and large front staging area.

Classroom Geography Can Help Create Equality

A classroom that is properly laid out encourages equal student participation; one that is poorly laid out usually favors only motivated students.

- Recognize the classroom management advantages of this layout. You now have not one but four front rows. Front rows are excellent places to put students who need extra attention. Because your rows are shallow—usually no more than three or four desks deep—it will be difficult for students in the back row to be disengaged. Also, this layout gives you more room to move around the classroom and stand next to any student in a matter of seconds to give individual attention.

Selecting Powerful Images

An Interactive Slide Lecture begins with the careful selection of a few powerful images. Review the content of the lecture you will be giving. Note five to ten main historical points you want to make, and search for images to illustrate each of them. Look for images in textbooks, magazines, and coffee-table books that make a strong visual impact and will serve as visual reminders for your students. History "picture books," which are often oversized and usually carry page after page of glossy illustrations and photographs, can be found in your school or public library.

A successful Interactive Slide Lecture will run from five to fifteen slides for high school students and three to eight slides for middle school students. A few well-selected images that students take time to carefully "read" will have a far greater impact than a plethora of images recalling passive filmstrips of old. Look for images that

"Analyzing slides helps me to learn better because it's a window to the past and I can see through it."
High School Student

History Alive!

- are clearly tied to your teaching objectives
- illustrate key events, such as the bombing of Pearl Harbor
- graphically show human emotion, drama, suspense, or interaction
- have the potential for students to step into and act out
- are fun or unusual

Below are five slides from an Interactive Slide Lecture on the Vietnam War, along with the topic and the rationale for selecting that particular image among the great many available.

Topic: Review of French involvement in Vietnam

Selection Rationale: This map of French Indochina after World War II gives students a quick overview of how the Vietnamese have long resisted foreign domination. Maps, like this one showing distinct political boundaries and including a color-coded key, are excellent for broad overviews or introductions. They spark interest and discussion, especially if you have a student come up to the screen to point out details and to tie those details to your lecture.

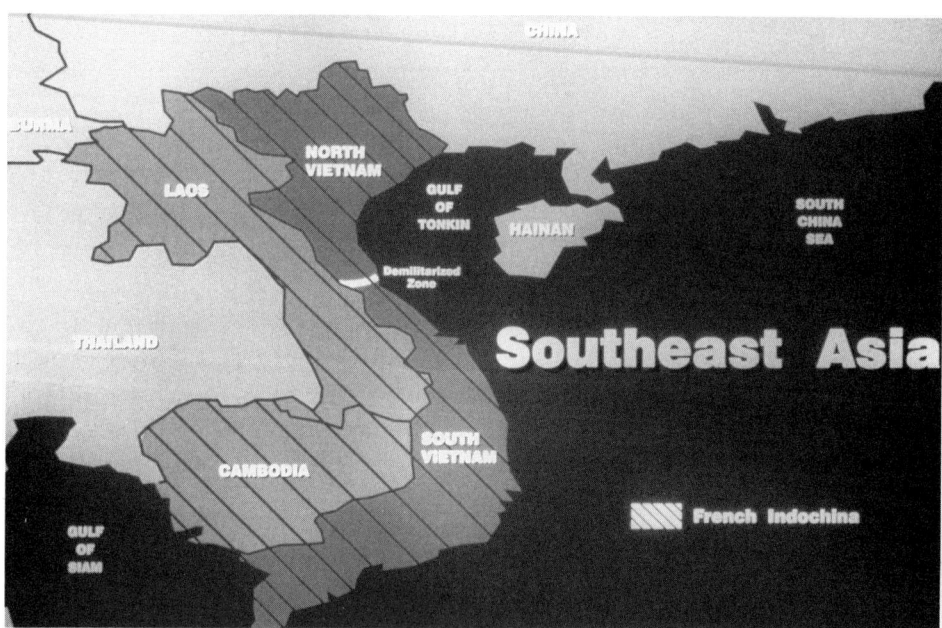

Topic: Buildup of U.S. combat troops in Vietnam

Selection Rationale: This slide of U.S. troops landing in Khe Sanh, South Vietnam, illustrates the massive deployment of U.S. troops. It is a strong visual reminder of the concept of deployment, and the heavily laden troops seem to be rushing into an uncertain future. This sets up an excellent opportunity for the teacher to assume the role of on-the-scene reporter and ask students who step into the slide what they expect to confront in the jungles of Vietnam.

Chapter 1

Topic: The moral dilemma faced by U.S. troops fighting a peasant army

Selection Rationale: This eerie painting, entitled "Charlie Subdued," of an American soldier and a Viet Cong prisoner in a rice field portrays the moral dilemma confronting many U.S. soldiers: the difficulty of knowing who the enemy was and why they were fighting a largely peasant army. This painting is a powerful primary source because it was done by a U.S. soldier. Asking two students to act out this slide and carry on a likely conversation between the G.I. and the prisoner has dramatic results.

History Alive!

Topic: U.S. troops adapting to guerrilla warfare

Selection Rationale: This photograph of a group of U.S. troops patrolling a river portrays the danger and hardship of jungle warfare. Students can be asked to place themselves in the shoes of these young men and then told two simple facts: most soldiers served a thirteen-month tour of duty, and their average age was nineteen. The teacher then reads from the diary of an American marine who wonders whether he'd gotten himself "out in the bushes for nothing," and the students are left with a lasting impression.

Topic: Choosing between Vietnam and the Great Society social reforms

Selection Rationale: This simple, direct political cartoon depicts Johnson's compromise of his Great Society reforms to fight the war in Vietnam. After the class interprets the cartoon, one student could stand in the slide, with a yardstick in one hand to represent the gun and a book in the other hand to represent the "butter" of the Great Society, and act out Uncle Sam. The class could try to persuade Uncle Sam to make the choice of holding either the guns or butter higher.

Chapter 1

'YOU MAY HAVE TO CHOOSE!'

Creating Questions That Lead to Discovery

For each slide, prepare a list of questions that spiral from the basic to the critical-thinking level. The slide is the primary source around which you will ask these inquiry questions.

One of the keys to a successful Interactive Slide Lecture is helping students to become visually literate. For example, if you want to teach about the humiliation and degradation depression-era families felt when taking government "handouts," you might choose an image similar to the one on page 32. Begin by having volunteers stand next to the projected image and physically point out the answers the class gives to basic questions you ask. Thus for the first question, "What do you see in this photograph?" the class should help the volunteer point to such items as the man unloading the truck, the sign reading "Federal Surplus Commodities," the line of sad-looking townspeople, the sacks of flour, and an African-American man at the back of the line. Make sure students stand to the side of the image and keep the pointer touching the detail for as long as the class discusses it. Students should not begin interpretation until they have identified all the visual details.

Students often immediately want to analyze images with comments such as, "These people have been standing a long time and are tired and bored" or "These are just the poor people in town getting their usual handout." While their interpretations may carry some truth, students will come to sounder conclusions if they slow down and notice all the details in an image. After students have identified the details in this photograph, for

"To say whether a picture is, or is not, by Bellini or Botticelli involves a combination of memory, analysis, and sensibility. Memory of facts and documents is replaced by visual memory."
**Kenneth Clark,
British Art Historian**

History Alive!

instance, they typically understand that these were once self-sufficient townspeople who are now ashamed at having to take government subsidized food.

Don't move to the next level of questioning until most of your students can "see the answers" to your questions. In this way, you will give students the building blocks they need to understand the most important historical concepts in each slide. Carefully tie each question into the questions preceding it. Your final questions may be at such a high level that only a portion of your class can answer them; this is okay. This questioning strategy allows all students to learn—students with low visual and linguistic skills are given the basics and those with higher skills are challenged. To keep student engagement high, show a new slide every five to fifteen minutes.

As students respond to each slide, incorporate their ideas into brief notes on the overhead projector. Have students copy the notes into their notebooks and add questions and details of their own. This is also your opportunity to give any pertinent historical information students were unable to glean from the slide. Since each slide illustrates a historical point about which students do not know all the details, your expertise is vital.

A Note About Notes

You may find it more effective to write overhead notes as you go along, rather than having pre-written notes, because you can include student comments about the slides.

"The slide lectures help me understand more about what we are studying; the class gives their ideas and it is more interesting looking at the slides than just studying the book."
Middle School Student

Here, townspeople line up to receive free food during the Great Depression. Spiral questions you might ask your students include:

- *What do you see in this photograph?*
- *What does the sign on the truck indicate?*
- *What are these people doing here?*
- *What feelings might these people be experiencing?*
- *Why aren't these people talking with one another?*
- *Why do they seem uncomfortable?*
- *Would people in need act the same way today? Why or why not?*

Chapter 1

Getting Students Involved

By the time students arrive in your classroom, they have been trained for years to sit passively and listen. Being asked to stand in front of the class to touch a slide or to act out what they think is happening can come as quite a shock. Some teachers are concerned that students might refuse to act out what they think is happening or might declare the strategy "ridiculous" and use peer pressure to convince others not to participate. Some teachers fear they will lose control of the classroom. Most students, however, are anxious to learn in new ways and appreciate alternatives to lectures. Take a few careful steps before showing your first slide to tap into this enthusiasm:

■ **Create a cooperative classroom environment.** First, and most important, do not attempt this strategy until you have created a cooperative, tolerant classroom environment (see Chapter 7). The students must know it is safe to take risks in your class.

■ **Make the first time a success.** The first time you ask students to come forward to touch a slide or to act out what they think is happening must be a success. Make sure the first few images you use are not so serious that laughter would be inappropriate. A photograph of trench warfare or an exploding atom bomb would not be ideal first images. Then, make sure your most daring students are in the first group you ask to come forward. Have fun with them; let them use humor and laughter to ease tension. Concentrate on getting them involved. Once you have established a precedent for student involvement, other students will follow happily.

■ **Get groups of students involved.** There is safety in numbers. Initially ask only self-confident students to step into the slide alone. Pairs work well when students are simply pointing to objects in an image—you can have each student stand on one side of the large screen and point to objects on that side. Larger groups work well for impromptu minidramas.

■ **Explicitly teach students how to interact with a projected slide.** Tell them to stand as near to the screen as possible. When they point things out, have them use a ruler or pointer and stand far to the side so they don't block the class's view. If they are engaged in an act-it-out, have them turn their bodies toward the class and address everyone clearly.

■ **Allow students who do not want to participate to pass.** Students must know that is okay not to participate—they may be having a bad day or suffering from stage fright. You may have one or two recalcitrant students who initially refuse to participate. By offering them the safety of being able to pass and by using your best powers of persuasion and humor, you will usually have them participating in a month or two.

■ **Model risk taking.** Since this strategy requires students to take risks, be willing to take risks yourself. Be energetic. Ham it up. For example, become one of the historical figures yourself and have students interview you. Students are more likely to take greater risks if you do. Today's students respect a teacher who dares to be different.

"At first I was afraid my eleventh-grade students would think they were too cool to do an impromptu act-it-out. So for my first slide, I picked three of the most popular kids and gave them a quick pep talk before class. They did such a great job and had so much fun that soon nearly all my students were vying to get involved."
Dottie Riffenburg,
High School Teacher

"My kids literally jump at the chance to step into slides. They like it so much that I receive unsolicited thank-you notes from them in their notebooks—thanking me for allowing them to participate instead of just listening, for letting them look at the slides and take notes at the same time, for allowing them to have fun while they learn."
Cathy Belcher,
Middle School Teacher

History Alive!

Here students step into a slide of a bank rush during the Great Depression and act out what they think the angry depositors would be saying. To encourage student involvement like this, create a cooperative class environment and clearly state your expectations.

■ **Be prepared to correct historical inaccuracies.** When students point to things in a slide or act out what they think is happening, they will say and do things that are historically inaccurate. Note inaccuracies and then, when you are writing down notes on the overhead projector, correct them. You will turn an inaccuracy into a learning experience. Had you stopped students in the middle of their impromptu act-it-out to correct an inaccuracy, you might have inhibited further response. As your students become more uninhibited, however, you might attempt to correct inaccuracies as they come up.

■ **Encourage students to act out the scenes.** Some slides may be appropriate for impromptu act-it-outs. These slides usually involve dramatic human interaction; for instance, a Russian poster showing slaves carrying the Czar. Ask volunteers to stand in front of the slide and "enter the image" as they act out what they think is happening. Ask them to put their bodies in the same positions as the people in the slide and to make the same facial expressions. Act-it-outs will bring several images in an Interactive Slide Lecture to life.

■ **Interview students.** A great technique for getting students to open up during act-it-outs is to conduct interviews with a fake microphone (a pencil or ruler works fine). Ask probing questions. If students say things that are historically inaccurate, challenge them to think deeper. If they say, for example, that they are "mad at the police for fighting in Vietnam," remind them that the officers are protecting the Pentagon, not fighting in the Armed Forces.

"Pictures show the story; notes only tell it."
High School Student

Impromptu act-it-outs are often tense and emotionally charged as students feel and appreciate the passions of the time. In this slide depicting the Vietnam War protest, you might have students take on the roles of protesters and police.

Chapter 1

Making Your Own Slides

Commercially produced slides or parts of old filmstrips are two sources of slides for Interactive Slide Lectures. Another, and many times far superior, source is history books with illustrations and photographs. Take these books to a professional photographer to be copied, or make the images into slides yourself. Here is a step-by-step method that will allow you to take slides and have them developed in a matter of hours—for a fraction of the cost of hiring a professional.

1. Purchase close-up lenses. You will need a single-lens reflex (SLR) camera with close-up lenses for this method. If you do not have close-up lenses, take your camera, along with the lens that came with it (the standard lens, typically 50 mm), to a camera store. Bring along a book that contains a small picture you want to copy. Explain that you want to make slides from books and to see a set of close-up lenses. (These typically cost under fifty dollars.) Ask the clerk to show you how to use the lenses, and practice on the book you brought.

2. Consider alternative lenses. The most inexpensive method for close-up photography is to use close-up lenses, but you may also want to consider alternatives, such as extension tubes or a macro lens. Extension tubes are more expensive than close-up lenses and have no real advantages; a macro lens is much more expensive but is easier and quicker to use.

3. Mount the close-up lenses to the front of your standard lens. The close-up lenses screw on to the camera's standard lens (remove all filters beforehand). The close-up lenses are marked +1, +2, and +4, and can be used alone or in combination. The +1 lens will allow you to photograph an image about half a page in size. If you add the +2 lens to the +1 lens, you will be able to photograph an image about a quarter of a page in size. If you use all three lenses together, you will be able to photograph a 2-by-2-inch image. Try out the various combinations. Whatever is in focus in your viewfinder will be in focus in the slide.

4. Purchase 50 or 64 ASA film. Several types of film will work fine. Kodachrome will give you warm colors. Fuji Velvia will give you true colors. Polaroid slide film will cut out your processing time. Ektachrome is relatively inexpensive, and many color labs can process it within hours. Before you take in your film, call the lab and ask how long development will take.

5. Take your photographs in natural light. Taking slides outside doesn't work very well in the rain, but nearly all other weather conditions are fine; a cloudy day is ideal. It's best to photograph in the morning or afternoon; at noon you will likely get too much glare, and the strong light will result in washed-out colors. Place the book you are photographing on a table, with the sun in front of you so you do not cast a shadow on the image. Pin the pages down with large paper clamps. Hold the camera so that the face of the lens is as parallel to the image as possible. Find the combination of close-up lenses needed to get the image in focus, and adjust the f-stop and aperture as you would for a regular outdoor photo. If the photograph has a lot of white in it and your camera allows manual adjustments, close your aperture one or two settings. When everything is set, shoot the image.

Close-up lenses screw on to the camera's lens and enable you to take quality photographs from books and magazines.

Play with Your Close-up Lenses

The best way to become a close-up photography expert is to open a book to a page with photographs of different sizes and try to frame and focus on each different size. Use your close-up lenses in various combinations. Experiment and see what gives you the best results. Remember: The right combination of lenses is the one that gives you the image correctly cropped and in focus.

Beating the Lawyers: Copyright Considerations

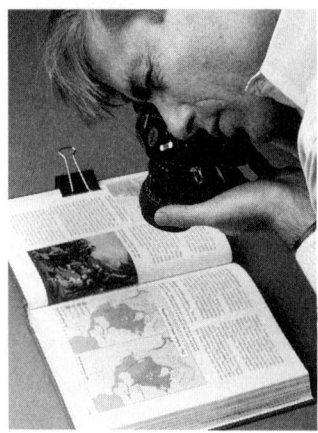

Making slides of copyrighted images for teaching purposes is considered fair use according to Section 107 of the 1976 U.S. Copyright Law. There are also guidelines in the interpretation of fair use that have been agreed upon by the Association of American Publishers and the Authors League of America that state that a single copy of a copyrighted work may be made by a teacher for use in teaching a class.

History Alive!

6. Label each image you photograph. Insert a self-adhesive note by each image you photograph. You may want to label it with the image's sequence number. As soon as you receive the developed slides, label each slide with the book, page number, and subject.

7. Store your slides in plastic sheet holders. Photography stores sell plastic sheets that fit into binders and hold twenty slides, an inexpensive and accessible way to store slides. By keeping binders of slides in your classroom, organized by topic, you can pull out a slide in a matter of seconds to illustrate an aspect of the lecture you are giving.

Three Outstanding Interactive Slide Lectures

The key to success for an Interactive Slide Lecture is to make the activity truly interactive. This requires a cooperative classroom environment, a bit of drama on your part, and some powerful images. Here are brief descriptions of three Interactive Slide Lectures that meet these criteria.

☐ The Economic Collapse

This Interactive Slide Lecture is part of a unit on the Great Depression. Students view and interact with eleven slides chronicling the causes and effects of the economic collapse of the late 1920s and early 1930s. The activity begins with a photograph of a billboard depicting American prosperity displayed in a poverty-stricken town. The image leads students to look at the serious economic problems underlying the seeming prosperity of the 1920s. The next group of slides depicts various symptoms of the economic collapse: a run on a bank, an abandoned farmhouse, an unemployed apple vender, a

Dramatic photographs, such as this one showing a group of unemployed steelworkers huddled around a fire in a "Hooverville" during the depth of the Great Depression, can turn a lesson about the causes of the depression into a memorable activity.

Chapter 1

man pleading for work, Americans lining up for free food, unemployed steelworkers in a "Hooverville." The last three images depict the inaction of Hoover and the election of Roosevelt. The final image is a political cartoon showing a confident Roosevelt taking over from a haggard Hoover.

Favorite Features

- Students take on the facial expressions and body language of destitute people.
- Strong photographs of poverty evoke empathy from students.
- Student act-it-outs are sad and touching.
- Students gain a better understanding of the complexities of poverty.
- Discussions about homelessness today are more sophisticated.

"Before we studied the Depression in this way, I thought people who were poor were just lazy. But when you see normal, hard-working people suddenly get all messed up by something they had no control over, it makes you think. Acting out what I thought was going through these peoples' minds made it stick with me way past the test."
High School Student

☐ The American Revolution Through Art and Music

The American Revolution comes to life in this Interactive Slide Lecture that uses paintings, engravings, and music from the Revolutionary period. Art is used not only as a visual representation of key events—the Battles of Lexington and Concord, Washington crossing the Delaware, a Revolutionary recruiting poster—but also as a means to analyze the contributions of unheard Americans. While the paintings do not highlight the contributions of women, African Americans, and Hispanic Americans to the cause of Revolution, students can be guided to look more closely at the works to decipher their

This well-known painting of George Washington crossing the Delaware River on Christmas Eve, 1776, pictures an African-American oarsman. It serves as a powerful visual reminder of the role African Americans played in the fight for independence.

"I used to show all of the paintings in this Interactive Slide Lecture and many, many more in a seven-minute filmstrip. The kids were bored stiff. Now I use eight slides interactively over two periods and the kids really get into it."
David Ellison,
Middle School Teacher

37

History Alive!

deeper meanings. For example, in Emanuel Leutze's painting, "Washington Crossing the Delaware," one of the oarsmen is an African American. This serves as a reminder that of the thirty thousand soldiers who fought for independence, about five thousand were African Americans. After analyzing the paintings, listening to Revolutionary War music will make the paintings and the event more memorable.

Favorite Features

- Students get to play art historians and look for hidden meanings behind paintings.
- Some paintings have fascinating histories of their own, such as Benjamin West's painting of the Paris peace conference, which was never finished because the British commissioners refused to pose.
- Students bring otherwise staid Revolutionary paintings to life by acting them out.
- Revolutionary War music combined with battle scenes makes this period memorable.
- Students enjoy probing for evidence of the contributions of women, African Americans, and Hispanic Americans in paintings that, at first glance, only contain European Americans.

☐ Ghana: The Kingdom of Gold

Middle school students often have naïve notions about Africa, especially Africa in the Middle Ages. This Interactive Slide Lecture challenges some of those misconceptions. Interacting with several slides that depict Ghana as a powerful and just kingdom, students discover that Timbuktu was not only a

Students gain an appreciation for the central role Timbuktu played in African trade as they analyze this picture of travelers entering the city after a trans-Saharan trek.

"Unless middle school students are actively involved in their learning, they won't remember much of what you teach them. Using this Interactive Slide Lecture I not only engaged my students, but gave them a new way of looking at the history of Africa. It worked."

*Terry Coburn,
Middle School
World History Teacher*

real place, but a complex city and thriving trade center during the Middle Ages. They see evidence that women were treated with more equality than they were in Europe at that time. Other slides show Ashanti weavers, a camel caravan, and advanced farming methods. Students learn that Africa was once a land of great kingdoms, and are encouraged to ask lots of questions: Why didn't I know any of this before? Why don't we get this image of Africa in the media? How did Europeans enslave people from such powerful kingdoms?

Favorite Features

- Challenges stereotypes and makes students think.
- Teaches students why salt was literally "worth its weight in gold" during the Middle Ages.
- Explains why Africans became Muslim.
- Shows how drummers communicated with drums, and creates a great opportunity for a fun drumming activity.
- Allows you to "lecture" to middle school students without boring them.

Strategy Two: Social Studies Skill Builders

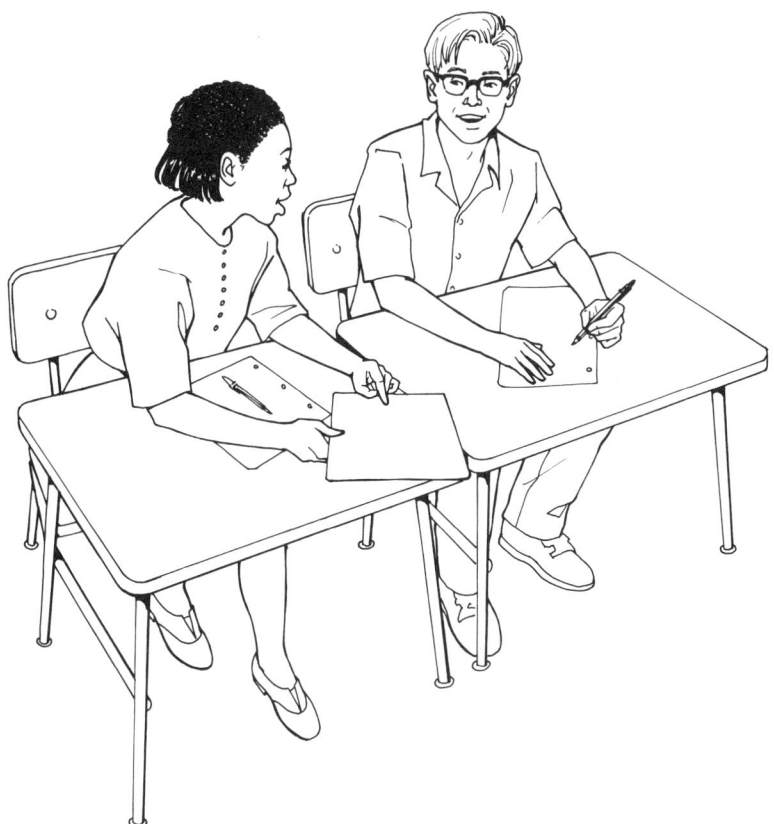

In this strategy, students work in pairs to complete fast-paced, skill-oriented tasks such as mapping, categorizing, interpreting political cartoons, graphing, identifying perspectives, and analyzing primary sources. The teacher begins an activity by quickly modeling the skill and then challenging students to practice that skill again and again. Students receive feedback as they work. The activity ends with a debriefing session, allowing students to use their new skill to gain greater insights into history.

Terry Coburn, a seventh-grade teacher, is passionate about teaching history—especially the often-ignored histories of Africa, Asia, and Latin America. Early in his career, however, he had a classroom experience that nearly extinguished his passion.

Terry carefully researched and delivered a week of instruction about the classic Mayan civilization that flourished in Mesoamerica six hundred years before the arrival of the Spanish. He told his class, a mixed group of European-American, Indochinese, African American, and Hispanic-American students, that the Maya not only had discovered the use of the zero, but also had developed a calendar more accurate than any in Europe at the time. Students were given an activity about the Mayan calendar that combined the skill of reading a time line with simple math skills.

"My students moaned and groaned about doing the skills lesson and told me that math had no place in a history class," Terry says. "Despite everything I had told them, they still wanted to believe the ancient Maya lived in rude homes, had no technical achievements, and led a boring life. The lesson just didn't work."

Although the lesson failed, Terry still believed that if his students could read a Mayan calendar, they would have a greater appreciation for the

History Alive!

"I realized that this lesson motivated my students to use and refine their social studies skills."
Terry Coburn

ancient culture. So he tossed out the ineffective worksheet and attended a lecture about Mayan astronomy. He learned more about the complex Mayan calendar and number system. He carefully studied the calendar until he understood it well enough to make a simple replica. His calendar had a large wheel on the outside with the names of the Maya's twenty days and a smaller wheel on the inside with thirteen Mayan numbers.

The next time Terry taught about the scientific accomplishments of the Maya, he told his students how the Maya had used their knowledge of astronomy to create their calendar. He divided students into pairs and gave each pair a copy of his Mayan calendar. The students quickly cut out the two wheels and attached them with push pins. Terry showed them how to line up the days of the week with the numbers to identify the first days of the Mayan calendar: 1 Imix, 2 Ik, 3 Akbal, 4 Kan.

"It was an exciting moment when my students understood how the two wheels functioned together to calculate a date," Terry says. "Many students learned the skill quickly and were ready to apply it. Others needed a bit more guidance."

Terry devised a method for giving immediate feedback both to students who grasped the use of the calendar quickly and to those who needed more help. He put a series of word problems on colored 3-by-5-inch cards. Blue cards challenged students to make simple calculations such as: Calculate the Mayan name of the seventh day on the calendar. Green cards had more difficult problems: Today is 5 Chuen. Your son went into town to obtain some farming tools. He left on 10 Oc. How long has he been gone? Students received immediate feedback and earned points for each question they answered. If they answered incorrectly, they were allowed to go back and discover the correct answer.

The lesson had not only given students the opportunity to use and refine their social studies skills while learning about the ancient Maya, but also to confront their stereotypes about native peoples. It was, in Terry's words, "a moment of classroom magic."

What Are Social Studies Skill Builders?

Teaching key social studies skills—mapping, categorizing, interpreting a political cartoon, graphing, reading a time line—is a vital part of any history course. Without these skills, students cannot fully grasp many historical concepts. Why teach students about the Proclamation of 1763 if they cannot find the Appalachians on a map? Why compare and contrast ancient Greece with imperial Rome without first teaching students how to use a simple matrix?

Despite the importance of teaching social studies skills, many instructors reserve little time and apply even less creativity to this vital task. In the words of one high school history teacher: "I don't have time to cover history *and* teach skills. Students should come prepared from the lower grades. Besides, when I do teach skills, my students say it's boring."

Social Studies Skill Builders are a special strategy for teaching skills. They turn traditional, rote tasks usually associated with worksheets into more dynamic, interactive tasks. Each task has these characteristics:

- Students sit in pairs to solve skill-oriented problems. Working with just one partner gives each student more opportunity to talk and to be involved than working in larger groups of four or five.
- Each task challenges students to use more than just linguistic abilities. For example, students might be asked to analyze a table about coal production and to connect what they have learned to a photograph of a coal mine, a task that uses logical and visual intelligences as well as linguistic intelligence.
- Each skill is introduced quickly, and students are challenged to practice it repeatedly. Active involvement is the key to success.
- Students are told exactly how their mastery of the skill will be assessed. For example, as students answer a series of questions, they are given immediate feedback—giving them incentives and creating a game-like atmosphere.
- Each skill lesson centers around important unit objectives. A lesson on analyzing propaganda posters from World War I, for example, might teach the principal causes of the war and give students the opportunity to practice important social studies skills.
- Each lesson is followed by a debriefing session with the entire class. Once pairs have struggled to analyze a series of World War I posters, they are eager to share what they have discovered and to learn more about the causes of the war.

"Working in pairs helps me because I get to explain my thoughts and get another opinion."
High School Student

Designing Social Studies Skill Builders That Engage Students

The key to designing an effective Social Studies Skill Builder is to craft your lesson so that the activity is inherently engaging. Here are five steps to help you create engaging skill lessons.

1. Choose your resources carefully. Select tasks for which you have readily available resources that can easily be developed into multiple-ability tasks. For an activity on analyzing World War I posters, you might begin by locating a collection of posters at your library. World War I posters are colorful, easy to reproduce, and depict both the Central Powers and the Allied points of view—enabling you to teach students how to look for bias. A collection of labor songs from the Great Depression, drawings of key inventions during the Chang Dynasty, or political posters from a presidential campaign could be the basis for an exciting lesson.

2. Have students use many different intelligences during the activity. For example, during the World War I propaganda activity, you might give each pair a placard with a reproduction of a poster. Pairs quickly sketch the poster, search for symbols, discuss the poster's meaning, and record their answers. Each time they analyze a poster they use linguistic, visual, interpersonal, and logical-mathematical intelligences. In another lesson, students could interpret excerpts from Thomas Paine's *Common Sense* by rewriting them in their own words and creating act-it-outs. To express Paine's assertion that there were no advantages to retaining a colonial relationship with

"I like these lessons because I get to do it enough times that I get really good at it. That way I earn lots of points and I remember the stuff better too."
Middle School Student

History Alive!

Great Britain, students might act out someone thinking thoughtfully for several seconds and then, with a shrug of the shoulders, walking away. This activity taps students' linguistic, intrapersonal, interpersonal, and body-kinesthetic intelligences.

3. Create a handout that encourages students to work as a team, but requires them to record information individually. In the World War I propaganda activity, each student in a pair could fill in a matrix after jointly discussing the poster. The matrix might have columns for recording the caption, describing the symbols, and recording interpretations. Each student will have a record of what the pair discussed and could use it to review for a test or as a resource for a culminating project.

Students analyze a series of photographs of Native Americans and use a matrix to note physical features of the land, Native-American adaptations, and hypotheses about which of several geographic regions the photograph represents.

In another Social Studies Skill Builder, students could apply their knowledge of the ways in which Native Americans adapted to the land by analyzing, with their partners, a series of photographs taken in the late 1800s. For each photograph, students would complete a handout noting the physical features of the land, pointing out how the Native Americans adapted to that area, and hypothesizing about which of several geographic regions the photograph represents. Writing down what they discussed helps students to be specific and to remember their ideas—and enables you to assess individual progress.

4. Create a set of durable placards to circulate around the classroom and give your students the opportunity for repeated, hands-on practice. The handout you create—maps, matrixes, lists of questions, or pieces of graphing paper—should have spaces for students to practice a skill many times. Each space should have a corresponding placard, which consists of visual or written information—a famous quote, a photograph with a caption, a primary-source document—that you've photocopied onto $8\frac{1}{2}$-by-11-inch card stock and inserted into a plastic sleeve.

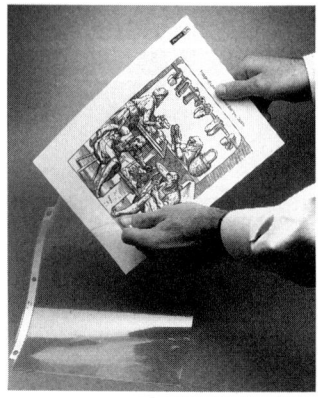

Making durable placards for Social Studies Skill Builders is as easy as photocopying illustrations, photographs, or text onto $8\frac{1}{2}$-by-11-inch card stock and inserting the copies into plastic sleeves.

For example, in an activity on graphing information about America's rising industrialism, students examine placards in pairs. Each placard contains an image and a line graph illustrating some aspect of industrialism in the early 1900s, such as the amount of raw steel produced or the miles of railroad track in operation. Using the information in the image and graph, pairs answer questions from a matrix on their handout. When they finish, they return the placard and their handout to the teacher for feedback. They then select a new placard and repeat the process.

In another activity, pairs examine placards with pictures of geographic challenges pioneers confronted along the Oregon Trail: the Great Plains, the Platte River, the Rocky Mountains, the South Pass, the Great Basin, the Blue Mountains, the Columbia River, the Willamette Valley. Pairs imagine how pioneers might have dealt with the obstacles and record their answers on a handout. Thus, students have several opportunities to practice a key geographic skill: predicting how geography affects human movement.

5. Design the activity to spiral from the basic to the complex, thus giving students deep historical insights during debriefing sessions. Structure Social Studies Skill Builders so students are challenged to answer progressively more complex questions. Through this step-by-step self-discovery process, students gain the building blocks they need to deal successfully with high-level, critical-thinking questions when you debrief the lesson. For example, in an activity on identifying multiple perspectives on slavery, pairs could analyze a series of placards, each with an image and written information about the views of a prominent historical figure: Frederick Douglass, Harriet Tubman, Sarah and Angelina Grimke, William Lloyd Garrison, Abraham Lincoln, Hinton Helper, John C. Calhoun, George Fitzhugh, or James Paulding. The objective is to show students there was much disagreement over the issue of slavery within the United States and that this was one of the many factors contributing to the tension between North and South before the Civil War.

The matrix students fill out could have three parts: 1. Record the person's name and state of residence. 2. Explain his or her view of slavery. 3. Describe the actions taken by the figure that support his or her view. This spiraling allows students to discover increasingly complex information before you debrief the lesson by holding a discussion on the multiple perspectives on slavery.

At the beginning of the class discussion, ask students to decide how to place the placards along a spectrum from people who were vehemently in favor of slavery to those who strongly opposed it. After students have sorted the placards, hold a discussion centering on such complex issues as: Was owning a slave ever justified? Which groups in the South benefited most from slavery? How did slavery affect the moral climate of our nation? Most students participate enthusiastically in this high-level discussion since they now have the knowledge base from which to expound about different perspectives. This is why spiraling questions from the basic to the complex is crucial: it allows each student to understand and articulate complex issues.

Teaching the Skill Quickly and Immersing Students in the Process

Introduce each Social Studies Skill Builder by quickly modeling the skill you want your students to practice. To captivate attention before you model the skill, consider challenging students with a statement such as: "I am about to teach you a critical social studies skill. You will need to master this skill if you want to earn points during the upcoming activity. But I only have seven minutes. If you don't listen carefully or if you distract me, you may not get all the information you need to master the skill."

Modeling consists of carefully explaining the steps your students must follow as they develop the skill. For example, here are the steps you could take to prepare students to label physical features on an outline map of the United States:

1. Give students an outline map of the United States. Have them point to north, east, south, and west on their maps, draw a compass rose in the southeast corner, and label the cardinal and intermediate points. Model this process by drawing the compass rose on an overhead transparency map projected on the front screen.
2. Write the term *physiographic feature* on the overhead transparency map. Ask students if they can define each word by itself and tell you what the concept means. Explain that *physio* means

Create Plenty of Placards

Plan to create at least eighteen distinct placards for each Social Studies Skill Builder you develop, one for each pair of students in a class of thirty six. If you do not have enough resources to create eighteen separate placards, make two of each placard. Having an adequate number of placards reduces the temptation for students to copy from their neighbors.

"Not only is this strategy effective in teaching students new skills, but it is designed to enable students to discuss high-level historical issues during the debriefing. After all the hands-on practice, students have a lot of information and opinions to share."

Bob Ruark,
Middle School Teacher

Model for Success

Whatever skill students are about to practice—reading a bar graph, analyzing political cartoons, creating an outline, interpreting primary source documents—the key to success is careful and thorough modeling.

"This strategy has changed how my students react to geography lessons. Instead of saying, 'Oh, we have to do another map,' they say, 'Great, we get to do something interesting.' Having them work in pairs creates social interaction that adds spice and allows them to share the burden on tough assignments."
Deborah Whitson,
High School Teacher

History Alive!

"physical," *graphic* means "written down or recorded," and *feature* means "a particular characteristic of something." Thus a physiographic feature is a physical characteristic of the land—such as a lake, mountain, or river—that is recorded on a map.

3. Tell students they will now use their geographic knowledge—location of the fifty states, basic terms, and the use of latitude and longitude—to answer a set of map-hunt clues. They will record the answer to each clue on their outline map by drawing in a physical feature such as a principal river, mountain range, or flatlands.
4. Show students how to create a key in the southwest corner, including symbols for open water, river, mountain, and flatlands.
5. Read a map-hunt clue to the class such as: What is the largest bay along the California coastline? Ask students to use their atlases to find the answer and to label the feature on their maps. Next, carefully label San Francisco Bay on the overhead transparency and put a symbol for water next to it.
6. Tell students they will now use the skill they just learned—labeling a physiographic map—to answer the map-hunt clues they are about to receive. Ask pairs to draw in rivers, mountain ranges, and flatlands as they answer each clue.

Preparing Students to Work in Pairs

After you have modeled the skill, it is time to place students in pairs. Because students will be discussing skill-oriented questions with discrete, defined answers, a group of two is ideal. Students will have more opportunity for interaction than in a larger group, and they won't run the risk of becoming disengaged. Here are some tips for preparing students to work in pairs.

■ **Divide your students into mixed-ability pairs.** Since the skill tasks are designed to require the use of the multiple intelligences, it makes sense to pair students with complimentary abilities. This will help ensure that each partner has something of value to contribute and that interaction is more equitable. Carefully assign students to mixed-ability pairs in advance of the lesson: put a student with strong linguistic skills with a student with strong visual skills, a logical-mathematical thinker with a body-kinesthetic thinker, or a musical-rhythmic learner with an interpersonal learner. Don't be surprised if it takes thirty or forty-five minutes to assign students to pairs. This is an art form; you will perfect your ability to create productive groups the more often you do it. You might consider keeping your students in pairs for at least two activities before reorganizing the groups.

■ **Before class, prepare an overhead transparency that shows who sits together and where.** On a permanent transparency, make a map showing the arrangement of desk pairs. Make sure your map encourages students to place their desks evenly around the classroom; if pairs are right next to one another, students will be distracted. With erasable overhead markers, write the names of students next to the desks at which you want them to work. This will help students find their partners and move efficiently into groups. Use the transparency as a template for your next Social Studies Skill Builder.

Chapter 2

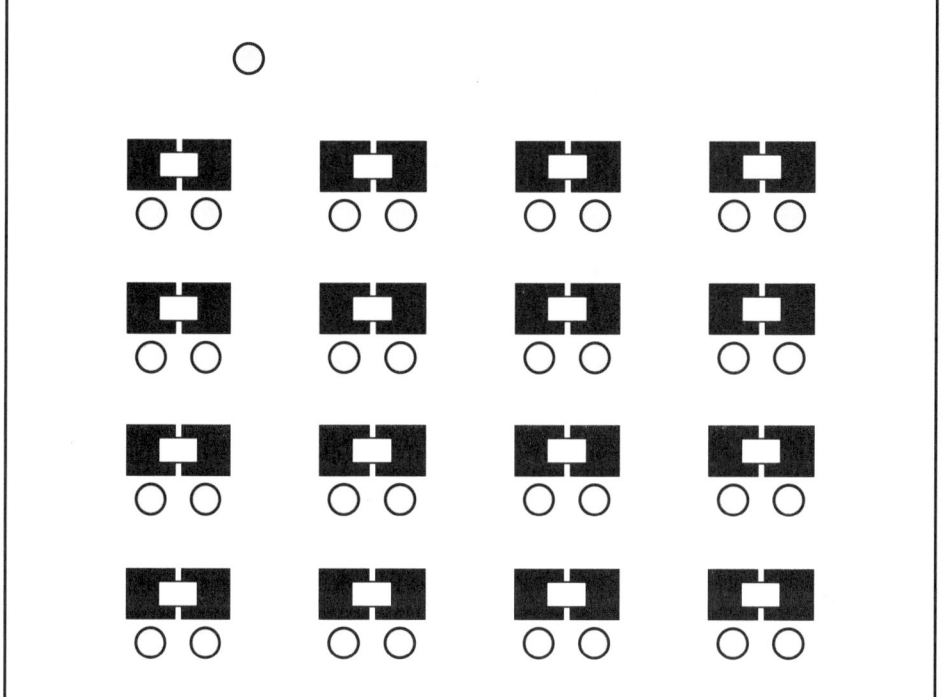

Place desks evenly around the classroom so that pairs can work side by side during Social Studies Skill Builders.

When students have found their partner and put their desks together, have them introduce themselves.

■ **Instruct students to sit side by side with the edges of their desks touching.** Project the transparency map for students to use as a guide for getting into pairs. Tell students they are not officially a team until the right edge of one desk is touching the left edge of the other desk and both students are facing forward. This will position them to work efficiently because they will be able to read together and have a good-size workspace.

■ **Encourage students to introduce themselves.** Once students have found their partner and put their desks together, tell them they will introduce themselves to each other by shaking hands and exchanging names. Choose one student and model this behavior. Smile while you do this and, if appropriate, use humor to break the tension. Some students will think introducing themselves is silly and will laugh nervously. Laughter will help ease tension and make the pairs work together more effectively.

■ **Do a quick ice-breaking activity to warm students up for working together.** An ice-breaker might be as simple as having students look directly into their partner's eyes as they, with conviction and spirit, repeat this statement: "Partner, if you need a helping hand, I'm here to help. And if I need a helping hand, I want you to extend one to me." Alternatively, you might ask them to spend a minute discussing a question such as "If I had a million dollars I would spend it on . . ." or "Over the weekend I think my teacher…" Students may find ice-breakers silly, but they will benefit from the few moments it takes to ease tension before they work together.

"At first I felt awkward asking my students to shake hands and repeat greetings when they moved into new groups. A few students did roll their eyes as if to say my request was ridiculous. But I noticed they remembered and used each others' names."

**Anne Maloney,
High School Teacher**

47

History Alive!

Setting Clear Expectations and Giving Immediate Feedback

After you have quickly modeled the skill and have placed students in mixed-ability pairs, clearly state what you expect from them so you can fairly evaluate their work. You may want to award points for each part of an assignment students successfully complete.

In an activity on the Constitution you could, for example, set clear expectations before students get their first placard by saying: "You will receive a placard with a constitutional question on it. Name the section of the Constitution in which you find the answer, and write your answer in a complete sentence. Bring the placard and your completed handouts to me. You will receive one point for naming the correct section and two points for writing a thorough and accurate answer in a complete sentence. If you have an incorrect or incomplete answer, you will have the option of redoing the question. When I have finished evaluating your work on one placard, I will give you another. Your goal is to finish as many placards as possible."

Checking student work and awarding points as students progress through the activity has several advantages. It motivates students to work quickly and accurately in a game-like atmosphere. It keeps them on task: you will quickly discover groups that are working inefficiently or not at all. It serves as a quality-control method: by giving students immediate feedback and closely evaluating their work, you can ensure high-quality products. And it gives you a break from taking papers home at night.

The greatest challenge facing teachers who give their students immediate feedback during Social Studies Skill Builders is managing the constant, and possibly overwhelming, flow of students waiting to have their handouts checked. If you have thirty or more students, you run the risk of making them wait in a long line for your attention. If students wait more than a minute or two, the strategy will quickly lose effectiveness. Here are a few suggestions for managing the crunch of students:

- Know what you are looking for. Familiarize yourself with the handout, and perhaps fill one out yourself as a key, so that you can quickly check each student's handout for key points.
- Don't feel obligated to read every word of a student's work; a quick read looking for salient points will serve your purposes fine.
- Give pairs more than one placard to work on at a time. If a line of more than two or three pairs forms at your desk, give the students at the end of the line another placard or two with which to work. You will find that correcting answers to two or three placards is more efficient than repeatedly correcting just one.
- Inevitably, one or two pairs will finish all placards ahead of the rest of the class. Ask these students to sit in the front and to use their completed handouts (assuming they received the total number of points) as guides to correct other students' handouts.
- Some teachers prefer circulating around the classroom and evaluating handouts as students are working. They find this less stressful than continually trying to keep the line of waiting students short.

"My students like Social Studies Skill Builders because they learn without pain. The game-like atmosphere gets them so involved in analyzing placards and writing answers that they hardly realize how much they are learning."
Mel Sandholm,
Middle School Teacher

"Social Studies Skill Builders really work in teaching students to analyze political cartoons. Having pairs working on interpreting a cartoon allows for self-paced discovery and ownership of what they are learning. I can immediately tell if students have mastered the skill by having them present their interpretations to me."
Bob Couper,
High School Teacher

Debriefing the Lesson: Making Historical Connections

Most teachers find that there comes a point during each Social Studies Skill Builder when most of the class, but not everyone, has finished working. It may be more effective to stop at this point and debrief the activity than to wait for everyone to finish. Following is a debriefing method that allows all students, even those who did not complete several placards, to learn the lesson's historical content. It requires that you make each placard into a slide or an overhead transparency before the debriefing.

After you have stopped the activity and collected the placards, place them on a table. Ask one student from each group to come forward, pick a placard that his or her pair would like to present, and sit down. Then show a slide or overhead transparency of each placard and quickly have the student who choose that placard come to the front and tell about it. The student might interpret a propaganda poster, explain a primary source quote, or label a map. By quickly reviewing all the placards in this way, all students will be exposed to their content.

Now it is time to challenge students to think holistically about the fragmented bits of history they have learned. Tell them to put the placards in order. For example, you might want them to put a series of placards depicting the events that led to the fall of the Roman Empire in chronological order. Or you might challenge them to put a series of Italian frescoes into groups according to artist

Instruct one student of each pair to come to the front and, holding the placard so the class can clearly see it, to stand in relation to the other students where they think the placard belongs. Expect students to disagree and debate. Turn this into a discussion in which all class members try to figure out how to order the placards. The students holding the placards can change their positions relative to one another as the discussion unfolds. The discussion should focus on helping students make sense of the fragmented history they learned during groupwork. Following are some ways you can challenge students to group themselves.

Political Spectrum

Draw a line on the chalkboard or put a piece of masking tape on the floor to represent a political spectrum. Label the two ends of the spectrum with terms such as *Conservative* and *Liberal* or *Totalitarian* and *Democrat*. Have students stand along the spectrum where they believe their placard best fits. For example, in an activity on foreign policies, students could read short scenarios of foreign-policy actions by different countries and decide where on a foreign-policy spectrum—between isolationism and imperialism—each scenario falls. At the conclusion of the activity, students come to the front and stand along a foreign-policy spectrum (a long piece of masking tape on the floor with *Isolationism* on one end and *Imperialism* on the other). If the class disagrees with their placement, students may move to another position. This procedure allows each scenario to be analyzed thoroughly and clarifies the assessment of the most difficult scenarios for all students.

"I like these activities because I always know right away whether my work is right or wrong. I don't have to wait a week to find out what score I got on the assignment."
Middle School Student

"Debriefing Social Studies Skill Builders with the entire class gives me a chance to make sure all students understand the history I want to teach. I've found that after they have worked in pairs, they have a lot of details and ideas to share as a class."
**Lorin Wright,
High School Teacher**

Putting Your Students on the Line

Give students clear instructions on how to stand and hold their placards when grouping themselves along a spectrum. Tell students to hold their placard against their chest a few inches beneath their chin and to be sure they are not standing in front of anyone else. This will help the rest of the class clearly see each placard and how it is grouped in relation to the other placards.

History Alive!

Values-Orientation Spectrum

Create a spectrum for students to stand along that represents value judgments. The poles of the spectrum might read *Community Interest* and *Individual Interest* or *Pro-choice* and *Pro-life*. Challenge students to place ideas or opinions along the spectrum. For example, students could explore the values behind Kennedy-era programs such as the Peace Corps and VISTA by analyzing a series of promotional posters. During the debriefing session, students place the posters along a spectrum between *Values Our Government Emphasizes Today* and *Values Our Government Does Not Emphasize Today*. Students quickly grasp how different the government's values appeared during the 1960s than the 1990s. This activity challenges students to connect the past to the present in a way that has a powerful impact and leaves a lasting impression.

Students explore the values behind Kennedy-era programs by placing a series of posters they have just analyzed individually along a values spectrum, helping them to connect the past to the present.

Moral Continuum

Challenge students to place the actions of individuals, groups, or nations along a moral continuum between such poles as *Ethical* and *Unethical* or *Expedient* and *Principled*. In one Social Studies Skill Builder, for example, students could explore and judge the American response to the Holocaust. First they analyze a series of placards that contain a photograph and written information about the response by some group in America—the Roosevelt Administration, the general public, Congress, youth, Jews, the media, the military, the State Department—to the Holocaust. Then they place the placards between two poles labeled *Just* and *Unjust*. This not only reviews the history of the U.S. response to the Holocaust, but also leads students to a much deeper understanding of the American response to Nazism.

Historic Chronology

A simple but effective way for students to arrange placards during a debriefing is to place a series of events or trends in chronological order. For example, students could analyze placards with paintings from the Middle Ages and the Renaissance. By placing the placards in chronological order, they can attempt to trace the evolution of artistic style from the Middle Ages to the Renaissance. They discover how a common theme, such as the Madonna and Child or the crucifixion of Christ, changes as it is interpreted first by Cimabue, then Giotto, then Botticelli.

Logical Categorization

Have students use their logical intelligence to sort placards by category such as attributing a series of quotes to their correct authors, classifying art by its historical period, or assigning a group of governmental programs to their correct administrations. For example, students could match key Cold War terms—socialism, totalitarianism, democracy, freedom, communism, equality—with a placard of a political cartoon. When you debrief this activity, students could first categorize the placards into two groups, American or Soviet, and then match the Soviet terms with the American terms, grouping socialism with capitalism and freedom with equality. Categorizing the terms gives students a fundamental understanding of these difficult historical concepts.

Three Outstanding Social Studies Skill Builders

☐ Analyzing Attitudes on Immigration Through Political Cartoons

This Social Studies Skill Builder is most effective when taught after an Interactive Slide Lecture covering some of the reasons immigrants left Europe, what happened to them during the transatlantic crossing and at Ellis Island, and what life was like for them once they settled in America. The slides tell the story of turn-of-the-century immigration from the immigrant's point of view. In the Social Studies Skill Builder, students are challenged to see immigration from a variety of perspectives by analyzing a series of political cartoons about immigration in the early 1900s.

Begin the activity by modeling how to interpret a political cartoon, encouraging students to look for such elements as irony, caricature, symbolism, provocative captions, exaggeration, and stereotypes.

Give each pair a placard of one of several political cartoons. Students make a quick sketch of the cartoon on their handout, and then pairs discuss a series of questions about the cartoon with their partner. Each student brings you the placard and completed handout to be evaluated. When most pairs have had a chance to interpret most of the cartoons, stop the activity, collect the placards, and tell students they will now choose a cartoon to present to the class.

Have one or two pairs come to the front of the classroom and, in front of a projected slide of the cartoon, present their interpretation. When all

"Social Studies Skill Builders enable me to teach my students crucial skills and then discuss complex issues during the debriefing sessions. After my students have analyzed placards, they have a lot to talk about because they have real ownership of the material."
Diana Ruark,
Middle School Teacher

History Alive!

Students as Cartoonists

After students learn to analyze political cartoons, have them create their own cartoons about related contemporary issues.

Political cartoons, such as this one showing the dangers awaiting recent arrivals during turn-of-the-century immigration, are an effective way to teach students to analyze and appreciate a complex issue from a variety of perspectives.

cartoons have been presented, collect the placards one more time and randomly pass them out again, challenging students to come forward and place their placard along a political spectrum between *Tolerant* and *Intolerant*. This leads to a high-level discussion about the political perspective of each cartoonist and shows students how immigration can be viewed from many different angles.

Favorite Features

- Uses a spiral design so students acquire the basic knowledge they need to answer progressively more complex historical questions.
- The political cartoons contain images—Uncle Sam as a tyrant, Europe as a demon, immigrants as scoundrels, the Statue of Liberty as a dump site for immigrants—that students find provocative and worthy of animated discussion.
- Because students must sketch each cartoon before discussing it, those with highly developed visual and artistic skills become very involved in the discussion.
- Many of the cartoons present enigmatic portrayals of immigrants that the students enthusiastically argue about from a variety of perspectives.
- Students appreciate the complexities surrounding immigration at the turn of the century and discuss current immigration issues with greater sophistication.

Chapter 2

☐ Discovering the Southwest Heritage

This activity could be used in a unit on Manifest Destiny to allow students to discover Mexicano contributions to the culture of the American Southwest. In pairs, have students examine a series of placards, each containing a 1950s photograph of some aspect of Southwestern culture—ranching, irrigation, adobe architecture, family life, blanket weaving—that dates back to the 1800s. Have students match each photograph with a corresponding descriptive paragraph, which are taped to the classroom walls. This allows students to move about the classroom as they practice the skill of reading for a purpose.

After students match the photograph with the paragraph, have them design a visual symbol for the contribution and place it on a map of the Southwest. Below the symbol they write a sentence that begins: "This contribution was important because. . . ." By the end of the activity, students have an illustrated map showing several separate cultural contributions Mexicanos made in the Southwest.

During the debriefing session, challenge students to place the placards along a spectrum between *Mexicano Contributions We See in Our Community Today* and *Mexicano Contributions We Do Not See in Our Community Today*.

A series of photographs depicting Mexicano contributions to Southwest culture, such as this one of a Mexicano mule driver showing a European American how to pack a mule, can give students an appreciation for Mexicano culture.

History Alive!

Favorite Features

- Matching the photograph with a descriptive paragraph taped to a wall keeps kinesthetic learners involved in the lesson because they are constantly moving around the classroom. It is also a powerful way to entice visual learners into using their linguistic skills.
- Putting the symbols for cultural contributions on a map of the Southwest challenges students to use visual and logical-mathematical skills and reinforces their physical geography skills.
- Teaching this activity puts the Mexican War in perspective and dispels myths students have about the Southwest being a land empty of people and devoid of culture before the arrival of European Americans.
- By telling students you cannot think of how any of these Mexicano contributions still survive today, you play the role of devil's advocate during the debriefing. Students will enthusiastically disagree with you and cite examples in their community to prove their point.
- Teachers report that students vehemently debate the affects of Mexicano culture on U.S. culture and, in the words of one teacher, "students are surprised when they learn about many influences they had ever dreamed existed."

☐ The Widening Struggle: Analyzing Civil-Rights Documents

In another activity students could explore how the actions of African-American civil-rights leaders during the 1960s encouraged other groups of Americans to seek justice and equality. Have students sit in pairs to analyze placards, each containing an image and a primary source reading, that illustrate how eight different groups—the Black Panthers, the United Farm Workers, gay-liberation activists, black nationalists, Native Americans, the Student Nonviolent Coordinating Committee, white civil-rights workers, and women—fought to secure civil rights in the 1960s and early 1970s.

After students examine each photograph and read the corresponding material, have them complete a matrix that requires them to do three things: 1. List examples of the kinds of discrimination the group was fighting against. 2. Describe the methods and strategies the group employed to gain civil rights. 3. Sketch a simple flag that uses symbols, color, and words to represent the values of the group simply and clearly.

Debrief the activity by showing a slide of each placard and having pairs tell the class what they learned about that particular group. Then randomly pass out the placards to individual students who, with the help of their partner, decide where the group on their placard would fit on a spectrum between *Radical* and *Conservative*.

Students can analyze documents from the civil-rights movement, such as this poster advertising a conference held in 1966 by the National Organization for Women.

Chapter 2

Favorite Features

- The flag students sketch for each civil-rights group serves as a powerful visual mnemonic to help them remember that group's goals.
- This activity honors the accomplishments of African-American civil-rights leaders by showing how they influenced the broadening struggle for equal rights.
- Students take on the role of historians as they analyze primary source photographs and documents to assess the accomplishments of each group.
- This activity teaches a large body of history in an academically honest yet brief lesson.
- This activity helps students distinguish obvious and subtle differences between the strategies of different civil-rights groups.

"This activity shows just how many groups participated in the civil-rights movement."
High School Student

CHAPTER 3

Strategy Three: Experiential Exercises

This strategy taps into intrapersonal and body-kinesthetic intelligences to allow students to feel the drama of the past. Usually one class period in length, Experiential Exercises recreate historical moments, events, and circumstances. Students are placed in historical situations—such as a trench on the western front in 1918, a turn-of-the-century assembly line, or an American colonial town meeting. Students react to these experiences as if they were individuals of the time, gaining an appreciation of history as a compelling human drama.

For several years, Connie Davidson attempted to make her eighth-grade students understand and appreciate the efforts of nonviolent protesters during the civil-rights movement. Connie, an African American, hoped her students would be moved by the courage of civil-rights workers and inspired to learn more about them. Year after year, she prepared lessons in which her students read well-chosen primary source accounts, saw compelling video clips, discussed the philosophy of Martin Luther King, Jr., and kept journals as if they were nonviolent protesters. Despite her efforts, Connie recalls, students remained largely indifferent to the actions of the civil-rights workers. "Even the video clips seemed unreal to them because they were in black and white. To them, these were faceless historical people who did something weird a long time ago."

Connie was convinced she needed a lesson that would make the movement more real. Rather than just having students read, watch, talk, and write about nonviolent protesters, Connie decided bring to life a lunch counter "sit-in." She prepared thirty-two role cards, each containing a description of a character students would assume during the activity.

On the day of the sit-in, Connie was cautious. "I prepared the lesson carefully, but I was still pretty nervous. The students had only a brief introduction to nonviolent protest when they watched a video clip the day before. I wasn't sure how they were going to react."

Students took one look at the transformed classroom and knew they were in for a different learning experience. A row of desks had become the lunch counter, complete with napkins and utensils; the rest of the desks formed a small jail in one corner. On the wall near the lunch counter

History Alive!

hung a sign reading Whites Only. Connie explained that they were going to recreate a lunch counter sit-in, like those in the South in the early 1960s. "Some students thought I was crazy. But others were excited."

Students were randomly given a role card, which assigned them a character and provided general parameters for how their character was to act and respond during the demonstration. The different characters met in groups—four police officers, three restaurant personnel, fifteen African-American nonviolent protesters, ten European-American townspeople—and were given five minutes to review their characters' beliefs. Police officers, for example, were to uphold segregation laws by arresting any African American who sat at the counter. Nonviolent protesters were to ignore or respond kindly to critical comments, to refrain from using violence under any circumstances, and, if arrested, to leave passively and peaceably. Restaurant personnel were to refuse service to African Americans and to call the police if they did not leave. Townspeople were to heckle and look scornfully at the protesters, though they were expressly told not to use racial slurs.

Once students understood their roles, Connie had them begin. Six protesters sat at the lunch counter and tried to order. As the police waited near the jail, townspeople began gathering to watch and heckle. The waitresses and restaurant manager refused to serve the African Americans and called the police. As police arrested the protesters—charging them with violation of segregation laws—and took them to jail, townspeople hurled insults. New protesters assumed the vacated seats.

As the sequence unfolded, Connie played an on-the-scene reporter, intermittently asking various characters to react to the goings-on. She was struck by the seriousness of her students. "When I asked a number of the characters how they were feeling or why they thought this protest was occurring, their answers were, for the most part, historically accurate."

Within twenty minutes, the jail was filled with protesters. Connie stopped the activity and debriefed the class. "This was the most exciting part of the lesson. Students experienced the real emotions of the moment, and most of them couldn't wait to share their reactions." Many recognized the depth of conviction it took for activists to commit to nonviolent protest in the face of hostility and pointed out that the activists of the time faced much graver hostility, including physical violence. The power of nonviolent protest was felt especially by the students playing the police officers and townspeople. No matter what they said or did, the protesters did not respond, which many students reported made them feel powerless. Some even realized the logistical problems that mass jailings created: "They couldn't just keep arresting everyone. What were they going to do when the jails filled up?"

For Connie, the experience was exciting. "It was a joy to watch them learn so much in such a short time. Putting students in the historical shoes of the civil-rights activists made them realize the courage and righteousness of these individuals. They had little way of understanding that otherwise." Afterwards, students were eager to learn more about the civil-rights movement. "All I heard for days after that lesson was, 'When do we get to do something like that again?'"

"Students experience the real emotions of the moment, and most of them couldn't wait to share their reactions."
Connie Davidson

"There are many truths of which the full meaning cannot be realized until personal experience has brought it home."
John Stuart Mill

Chapter 3

How Students Benefit from Experiencing History

In the conventional classroom, students don't learn history, they memorize it. History is presented—by teacher and textbook—as a series of names, dates, and facts. Some students are adept at memorizing these; most are not. But even students who memorize well generally do not retain the information longer than it takes to regurgitate it on a test. Fewer still are able to demonstrate at the end of the course any real understanding or appreciation for the effect history has had on their own lives. Lost in most conventional classrooms is the rich human drama of history, the compelling experiences of the individuals who shaped it, and the connections between the past and events today.

Experiential Exercises are one way to combat this problem. By making history come alive for students and allowing them to experience past events, true learning—interactive, memorable, and lasting—takes place. The benefits of having students "experience" history are many.

- **Experiential learning is motivating and memorable.** Typically, what occurs in classrooms across the nation, regardless of the subject, is remarkably similar: teachers talk, students sit and listen. Predictability is the cornerstone of the student experience. With Experiential Exercises, students are engaged in simulations or reenactments of historical events. Because these activities are different and unpredictable, students are aroused and motivated to learn.

- **Students use body-kinesthetic and intrapersonal intelligences to learn historical concepts.** Experiential Exercises generally tap into two of Howard Gardner's intelligences that are often ignored while teaching history: body-kinesthetic and intrapersonal. The activities are engineered expressly to evoke an emotional or physical response.

- **High-level concepts are made accessible.** Experiential Exercises strive to make the difficult concepts that are central to a period of history comprehensible. Sometimes key concepts are too abstract to simply be explained. By allowing students to experience the feelings that encompass an idea, high-level concepts can be made concrete. For example, after students have simulated working on an assembly line, they can more effectively understand alienation in an industrial society.

- **Experiential Exercises provide a referent throughout a unit.** An Experiential Exercise can be used not only to teach a specific concept, but also can serve as an ongoing referent throughout a unit. When students have a memorable experience learning about a topic—such as compromise, discrimination, or taxation without representation—you can draw on that experience as you teach related topics.

- **Students' reactions to Experiential Exercises create teachable moments.** In most conventional classrooms, teachers shy away from creating rich experiences for fear they will "lose control" over student reactions. Tapping into the drama of history and the feelings of individuals involved in past events threatens the calm predictability of the class and may produce unwelcome tension. Precisely because history is dramatic, loaded with emotion, and controversial, students need lessons that enable them to experience the

---

"The best thing about this class was learning through experience and activity, not from an ink-blotched, dead tree."
High School Student

Tell me, I'll forget. Teach me, I'll remember. Involve me, I'll understand.
Ancient Proverb

"Much of what we remember is carried as images, especially memory charged with emotion."
Gabriele Lusser-Rico

History Alive!

passion of past events. Well-crafted Experiential Exercises create teachable moments—instances in which students' senses and emotions are heightened and poignant conclusions can be made.

Preparing Students, Administrators, and Families

Experiential Exercises are risky because you cannot always control students' responses. The fundamental goal is usually to provoke an emotional reaction to a historical situation. Strong emotions—frustration, joy, anger, fatigue, apprehension, empowerment, passion, fear, camaraderie—surface during these activities. Sometimes student reaction is predictable; often it is not. Take the appropriate steps to ensure that students, administrators, and families are prepared.

Preparing Students for Experiential Exercises

■ **Create a cooperative, tolerant classroom.** Students will feel safe to react freely to these activities if they feel the class is a supportive community.

■ **Develop a trusting relationship with your students.** Once trust is established, students will take risks and willingly participate.

■ **Make sure the activity is appropriate for your students.** Consider the make-up and maturity level of your students before using an Experiential Exercise. Some teachers, for example, chose not to use an activity on World War I trench warfare during the Persian Gulf war because many students had friends and relatives fighting overseas.

Preparing Administrators for Experiential Exercises

■ **Explain your rationale for using Experiential Exercises.** Administrators need to know that you are using these activities for sound pedagogical reasons. Meet with them to explain why you are using this approach. Express any concerns you have about student reaction and be sure you have your administrators' full support.

■ **Invite administrators into your class during Experiential Exercises.** Allowing administrators to experience how your students are learning enables them to understand the power of these exercises. Teachers report that having administrators in the classroom also helps them gain support for this type of teaching and leads to greater school-wide collegiality.

■ **Enlist administrators' support in dealing with concerned families.** Explain that Experiential Exercises may cause concern among families who are not familiar with the unconventional nature of the activities. Knowing this, administrators will be better prepared to address concerns.

Preparing Families for Experiential Exercises

■ **Explain your rationale for using Experiential Exercises.** Use family night or a letter home to explain your rationale for using this teaching method. In most cases, parents will appreciate that their child will be challenged, interested, and engaged in activities in your class.

Dare to Risk

It's better to take a risk and fail than to pass out another worksheet.

"Whatever you can do, or dream you can, begin it. Boldness has genius, power, and magic in it."
Goethe

- **Invite families into your class during Experiential Exercises.** Urge families to attend class and to participate. While this initially may be uncomfortable for both parent and student, this rare, shared experience often sparks ongoing dialogue about the day-to-day class activities between students and their families.

- **Involve families in homework assignments related to Experiential Exercises.** After students spend the class period on an assembly line mass-producing a picture, for example, have them interview family members about their experiences working on assembly lines or in other repetitive or tedious jobs. Assignments like these foster better communication between students and families and help students see connections between history and their world.

When It Is Best to Use Experiential Exercises

Experiential Exercises awaken students to the richness, drama, and reality of the past. However, not every historical event or concept works well with this approach: Experiential Exercises must be used selectively. As you plan lessons, use Experiential Exercises when:

- **You can recreate a historical event or experience easily.** Most courses demand that you teach a large body of history in a relatively short time, so it makes sense to design activities that are easy to implement. Although recreating World War I trench warfare in your classroom may seem daunting, you can transform your room into a simulated battlefield within ten minutes. Move desks into two sets of two rows on either side of the room, and have students crouch in opposing "trenches." Project slides from the Europe's western front, and bang a ruler against a trash can to create the sights and sounds of the battlefield. Read passages from *All Quiet on the Western Front,* and have students react to situations in the novel as if they were soldiers. The result will be rich experiential learning with economy of time and energy.

- **Your teaching objective centers on a topic that is best taught through body-kinesthetic or intrapersonal intelligence.** Some history lessons are best taught through physical or emotional experience. The tedium, physical strain, and dehumanizing nature of assembly-line work, for example, cannot be communicated adequately through readings or slides: students must *feel* its physical and emotional effects. In an activity designed to allow students to experience the assembly line, muscles ache and minds wander as students spend a class period mass-producing a drawing of a human figure, each student specializing on one body part. By performing a repetitive task, students gain a wealth of knowledge—through body-kinesthetic and intrapersonal learning—on the merits and weaknesses of mass production.

- **You want to evoke an emotional response so that students emphatically react to the plight of individuals or a group in history.** Experiential Exercises can be used to increase students' empathy for victims of historical calamity by tapping into their intrapersonal intelligence. For example, students have a difficult time understanding the devastation of people who lost their savings when the banks failed during the Great Depression. They

"I heard about the real-life experiences my daughter was having in class. She was so involved and invested in the experiential activities that she wanted to share them with me."
Meg Sanders, Parent

"When I've talked to my students long after they have graduated from high school, what they remember most about my class are the dramatic Experiential Exercises we did. They leave a lasting impression."
**Ken Holmes,
Middle School Teacher**

I recreated pioneers moving west in an Experiential Exercise by using shopping carts as wagons as we moved west across campus. I used a steep staircase to approximate the Sierra, and a ramp leading down into the library as the dramatic descent out of the Sierra. Students across the campus saw what we were doing and wanted to be a part."

Harold Crumpley,
High School Teacher

Students feel a sense of pain and loss when a trusted institution—the teacher—loses their quizzes and cannot award them points. The class later discusses how this experience relates to emotions felt by bank depositors who lost their life savings during the Depression.

History Alive!

become much more empathetic after an activity in which they can experience the pain of a failing economy. This activity centers around students earning points on a quiz taken the previous day and then being told that half of their quizzes were "lost"—misplaced, inadvertently thrown away, or stolen. Those students whose quizzes were lost are told they will not receive points. After allowing students to react and voice their incredulity, the teacher debriefs the class and draws parallels between the students' feelings and those of victims of the bank collapse. In both cases, a trusted institution (the teacher's grading system and the banks) loses something of extreme value (points and money). This intrapersonal experience gives students insights that otherwise would have gone untapped.

■ **You want to emphasize how a historical occurrence affected the way people felt or reacted.** For students to understand the behavior of individuals in history, they must appreciate the conditions that shaped it. Students cannot comprehend the actions of Nazi Germany citizens until they recognize the deep-seated anti-Semitism that existed in Europe for centuries. Nor can they appreciate the radicalism of 1960s youth without understanding the generational conflict that existed between parents and youth. Experiential Exercises can replicate historical conditions so students respond in ways similar to those of individuals in the past.

To understand McCarthyism, for example, students must have an appreciation for the fear of Communism and paranoia of the time. An Experiential Exercise could create a situation analogous to the dread of being labeled a communist. Each student receives a slip of paper, either blank or containing a dot, and must move about the room trying to form the largest "dot-free" group while relying only on questioning and suspicion. Afterwards the teacher draws parallels between the fear of dots and the resulting classroom behavior, and the fear of communism and the rise of McCarthyism.

■ **You need to capture a moment or feeling that is central to understanding a historical period.** Some concepts are so central to understanding a historical period that unless students truly grasp them, they gain little from your teaching. In teaching the American Revolution, for example, you must continually refer to the concept of *taxation without representation* because it impacted nearly all aspects of the period. Students need a powerful, indelible understanding of taxation without representation to fully comprehend the motivation behind the revolutionary movement and the formation of the new government.

In an Experiential Exercise you could inform students that budget constraints have made it necessary for all students to pay ten cents per page for photocopied handouts, including the day's two-page quiz. As you attempt to collect this "tax," students will voice outrage and injustice—not unlike the feelings experienced by colonists prior to the Revolution. As students learn about the Sons and Daughters of Liberty and the Continental Congress, they can draw on how they felt about "unfair taxation" to better appreciate colonial motivations for forming protest organizations. And as students study the formation of the new government, they can be reminded of this experience to help them appreciate the colonists' desire for a representative government.

Chapter 3

How to Teach Experiential Exercises

Experiential Exercises require many of the same teaching skills—elegant lesson design, classroom preparation, clear communication, effective classroom management, sensitivity to students' feelings, facilitating discussion, and helping students reach conclusions—that other pedagogical approaches do. However, they require that you use all these skills in a short period of time—usually one period or less. The following guidelines will help you teach memorable and effective Experiential Exercises.

1. Keep activities simple and short. As you conceive of Experiential Exercises, try to rely on readily available classroom resources such as the chalkboard, desks, butcher paper, tape, and a slide projector. Limit each activity to one class period or less when possible; experiences that are immediate and concentrated are generally the most powerful. Occasionally an activity—such as simulating a colonial town meeting or resolving the conflicts that led to the Civil War—will last longer than a class period, but most Experiential Exercises are simple and to-the-point.

Reenacting the transatlantic slave crossing, for example, takes few materials and little class time. Have students, their hands bound with tape, lay side by side in a "loose pack" on the floor, view slides of the stages of enslavement, and hear and respond to passages from Alex Haley's *Roots*. In a single class period and with materials indigenous to most classrooms, students learn about the inhumanity of enslavement.

2. Arrange the classroom appropriately. Many Experiential Exercises require unusual room arrangements. Set up the classroom before students arrive; if students must move desks, time is lost and students are distracted from the mission of the activity. For example, an activity to introduce Manifest Destiny from the Native-American perspective might require ten students to move away from their usual "home" in the class to a small, undesirable area partitioned by desks. Having these desks in place before students enter class is imperative. Not only does it save instructional time, but the strange classroom arrangement piques interest and readies students for the activity.

3. Communicate expectations. While students find Experiential Exercises unusual and often fun, it is critical that you set clear behavioral and learning expectations each time you use them. Students must know that each activity has a specific academic purpose. This is especially true in such activities as one in which students spend an entire class period as medieval monks performing various monastic tasks in complete silence. Without expectations for absolute silence clearly communicated, students often giggle and talk, undermining the activity. However, if the teacher unequivocally outlines the behavioral expectations and the objective, students assume their roles and remain silent and purposeful throughout the activity.

4. Give students clear directions. Most Experiential Exercises require students to participate in activities that are far different from those in the conventional classroom. As a result, students need precise directions to feel comfortable. More significantly, an activity might fail if a teacher gives unclear directions. Consider the "dot" activity that you just read about. The directions

"The Experiential Exercises we do really show us how it felt to be alive long ago. I was a serf and it felt bad to be in a lower class. It is good to do these activities because you see social studies in a totally different way—in a fun way and in a feeling way."
Middle School Student

"The closer my Experiential Exercises are to historical reality, the more my students like them. Now I don't hesitate to bring in props to really give the kids a memorable experience."
**David Anderson,
High School Teacher**

History Alive!

for this exercise are initially confusing to students. At the beginning of class, skilled teachers warn students that the procedures to the dot activity are complicated, clearly explain the directions, and encourage students to ask clarifying questions. They tell students that they will not answer any procedural questions after the exercise starts. By placing the burden of clarification on the students, questions are answered before the activity begins, and the exercise can unfold without interruption.

5. Anticipate student reactions. Because Experiential Exercises are designed to elicit emotional responses, you must be prepared for student reactions. When students sit in "trenches" for forty-five minutes, know that they will feel tired and cramped; when students assume the roles of colonists to debate independence, expect passionate, forceful arguing; when quizzes are "lost" to convey the impact of bank failures, expect students to feel angry and frustrated.

Also expect the unexpected. Students often react with different intensity to the same Experiential Exercise. In an activity designed to have students understand the weaknesses of the Articles of Confederation, for example, thirteen student groups are required to decide which three of five symbols—representing music, family, hobbies and sports, love and friendship, and education—should be included on a coat of arms symbolizing youth today. The coat of arms must be approved with the consent of nine of the thirteen groups. To simulate competing interests among the groups, each group is secretly told that they will receive bonus points if certain symbols are adopted. What students don't realize is that the activity is rigged. You have made sure that no possible combination of the five symbols can create a coat of arms on which more than nine groups can agree. The objective, then, is for students to understand a fundamental weakness of the Articles of Confederation. Predictably, most students feel frustration as the class is repeatedly unable to agree. But sometimes frustration boils over into heartfelt anger. Prepare yourself for the unexpected, or it may be difficult to diffuse a potentially volatile situation.

6. Recognize teachable moments. Experiential Exercises produce teachable moments—instances when an activity evokes in students a feeling that someone in the past might have had. Recognizing and taking advantage of these moments is paramount to helping students grasp key concepts. Keep your learning objectives clearly in mind as each activity unfolds.

A skilled teacher would recognize a teachable moment in an Experiential Exercise designed to allow students to feel the intensity of conflict between the North and the South and to discover how difficult it was to avoid civil war. In this activity, students assume the roles of Northerners and Southerners and attempt to resolve the conflicts facing the United States in 1820, 1850, 1857, and 1861. When students try to reach an agreement about the future of slavery in 1861—sectional tensions are high after already haggling over three compromises—patience wanes and tempers flare. The teacher allows arguments between Northerners and Southerners until they reach a crescendo, then stops the exercise and asks students to write their response to the question: Why do you think the Civil War was fought? At this moment, students have insight—based on their own attempts to compromise—into the

---

Keep It a Secret

When you plan to conduct an Experiential Exercise in more than one class that requires an element of surprise, use humor to convince your students not to tell their peers about the activity. Have them raise their hand and repeat this oath: "In the interest of educational quality and excellence, I hereby swear not to reveal what happened in today's activity until the end of the day."

"Experiential Exercises generate a new level of energy and excitement in my classroom. Many of my students who usually aren't into history get turned on. The other day a student walked into class and said, 'What adventure do you have in store for us today?'"
Mike Warner,
High School Teacher

difficulty of reaching an agreement in 1861 and how the nation could go to war with itself.

Debriefing: Connecting the Experience to History

Experiential Exercises create rich, memorable experiences. For meaningful learning to occur, these activities must be skillfully debriefed so that students can talk about their feelings and relate their experiences to history. The debriefing process is critical and threefold: it allows students to express their feelings about the experience, to make connections between the experience and history, and to discuss how the experience differed from historical reality.

Allow Students to Express Their Feelings About the Experience

Experiential Exercises are designed to let students experience feelings similar to those of individuals in the past. Before you can make connections between the activity and historical reality, however, allow students to focus on the *affect* of their experience. Prompt them with this single question: What feelings did you experience during this activity? This question serves three purposes:

- **Students are encouraged to identify and articulate their feelings.** Some students, particularly those with weak intrapersonal intelligence, have difficulty identifying and describing their feelings. Having the initial portion of the class discussion focus on the affect of an Experiential Exercise helps all students better understand how they reacted.

- **Students are able to share their feelings in the proper environment.** In a cooperative, tolerant classroom, students feel safe to talk freely and honestly about how they felt and reacted. If this is not done in the classroom, students' emotions may spill over into other classes or at home.

- **Students know that their reactions are okay.** Letting students discuss their feelings without judgment sends them a powerful message: it is okay to have and share powerful emotions. This validation will set the foundation for the rest of the debriefing.

Make Connections Between the Experience and History

Once students have discussed their feelings, parallels between the Experiential Exercise and history can be made. Prepare carefully sequenced questions that enable students to draw connections between their experience and key historical concepts. Spiral the questions, from basic to higher-order thinking skills, so students can use their experience to understand key concepts. The questions should help students reach historical conclusions on their own; do not supply your analysis until students have been challenged to make their own conclusions. Consider, for example, the nature and the sequence of questions that could be used to debrief the assembly-line activity:

- What feelings did you experience during this activity?
- Describe the kind of work you did on the assembly line.
- How does this compare with drawing a picture on your own?

"I used to have no feeling about history at all. After doing these activities I really feel something. That helps me understand more about history."
High School Student

"Experiential Exercises put us into a time machine to experience the feelings of the past. It made me think a whole lot more."
High School Student

"The most important part of an Experiential Exercise is what happens after the experience. This is when I have to skillfully help my students make connections between the activity and the history we are learning. Without this, much of the learning can be lost."
Terry Coburn,
Middle School Teacher

History Alive!

- What made assembly-line work difficult? What made it desirable?
- How did you cope with the repetitiveness?
- How do you feel about the product you were producing?
- How do you think turn-of-the-century assembly-line workers felt about their jobs?
- Why do you think factory owners used the assembly line as a method of production?
- What are the positive aspects of mass production? What are the negative aspects?
- What methods other than the assembly line might be used to mass-produce goods?

A skillfully facilitated discussion centering on these questions has powerful results. Students can intelligently discuss the substantive issues surrounding the rise of industrialism—the drudgery of assembly-line work, the alienation of workers from the final product, the expediency and efficiency of mass production, the benefits of standardized products—for an entire period. And this occurs before they ever read, hear a lecture, or watch a movie about the Industrial Revolution.

Point out How the Experience Differed from Historical Reality

This final stage of the debriefing is necessary for students to gain a realistic understanding of a historical period. Center a discussion on this question: What were the major differences between what just happened in the classroom and historical reality? As students explore this question, they begin to see the differences in magnitude, scope, and seriousness between the classroom activity and historical reality.

Failing to do this after the activity on trench warfare, for example, would trivialize the experience of World War I soldiers. As students discuss the differences, they soon realize that the classroom experience could not approximate the grave issues soldiers faced: death, injury, starvation, filth, homesickness, intense fear. Similarly, the short time students are silent during the activity on medieval monks barely compares to the dedication of monks who sustained vows of silence for years or even decades.

Three Outstanding Experiential Exercises

The key to success with an Experiential Exercise is to bring to life a historical moment, event, or phenomenon. This requires your students' trust and a bit of risk taking on your part. It also demands that you consider experiential learning in a creative, new way. To help you adopt this mindset and to get your creativity flowing, here are detailed descriptions of three Experiential Exercises mentioned earlier in this chapter.

☐ Experiencing the Assembly Line

This activity, mentioned earlier, can be used in both world and U.S. history classes to teach about the rise of industrialism and mass production. Each student spends three minutes drawing a picture of a person. The class is then broken into two competing groups to replicate drawings of the best picture in each group. Each student specializes in drawing a particular part

Chapter 3

Students feverishly reproduce drawings to gain an appreciation for the monotony and rigor of assembly-line work.

Make 'Em Work

To approximate especially difficult working conditions, have students sit front-to-back so they must pass papers over their shoulders and work in isolation.

of the person—head, nose, shirt, legs—as the illustration is passed from worker to worker. Students' feel the physical, mental, and emotional stress of assembly-line work. Acting as the boss, the teacher urges the workers to speed up, to concentrate, to work harder. Some teachers even turn up the heat in the room, dim the lights, and seat students closer together to better approximate sweat-shop conditions.

Favorite Features

- Students develop empathy for the physical and emotional stress assembly-line workers experience.
- Discussion about the positive and negative aspects of mass production is substantive and sophisticated.
- Comparisons are made between cottage industry and the assembly line as methods of production.
- The activity provides an excellent segue into learning about unionization.
- Students are motivated to talk with their families about experiences in assembly-line jobs.

☐ McCarthy and the Cold War at Home

Students have tremendous difficulty understanding the conditions that allowed McCarthyism to flourish in an otherwise free society. This activity is used during the study of the Cold War to create an analogous situation to the fear of communism in America. Students receive a slip of paper that is either blank or has a dot on it and must keep their identities secret. The teacher instructs students to move about the room and to try to form the

History Alive!

Keep It Clear

Use the overhead to project the rules for the McCarthyism simulation so that all students know exactly what is expected of them as they form groups.

Students try to form dot-free groups as they simulate the fear and paranoia felt in the United States during the McCarthy era.

largest "dot-free" group. In determining who is a "dot" and who isn't, students must rely only on questioning and suspicion; they may not examine their classmates' papers. As students start to label classmates as dots, the conditions that produced McCarthyism—suspicion, unfounded accusation, demagoguery, guilt-by-association—emerge. Within minutes, the classroom is filled with fear of dots and paranoia about being associated with them. Afterwards, parallels are drawn between the wave of fear of dots and the resulting classroom behavior, and the fear of communism and the rise of McCarthyism. Students then move on to learn about this phenomenon and the subsequent downfall of Joe McCarthy in greater detail.

Favorite Features

- A difficult, abstract concept is made comprehensible.
- Students' curiosity about the topic is piqued by the uniqueness of the activity.
- A lively discussion about the motives for students' behavior during the exercise results.
- Parallels between McCarthy's methods and the student's actions during the activity are many.

☐ Living Trench Warfare

This Experiential Exercise can be used in either world or U.S. history classes to teach students about the physical and emotional trauma of World War I trench warfare. Desks are aligned into two sets of two rows three feet apart on either side of the room. When the bell rings, students are ushered into the opposing "trenches"—half as German soldiers and half as French soldiers.

Chapter 3

Students crouch in the crowded trenches, view slides of the battlefield conditions, listen to passages from *All Quiet on the Western Front,* and hear the sounds of artillery and machine guns. As this occurs, students are prompted to respond verbally, physically, and in writing to a variety of circumstances with which trench soldiers were faced. Afterwards, students write a letter to loved ones describing the experience.

Favorite Features

- Vivid historical images, literature, body-kinesthetic learning, and writing are elegantly integrated.
- Students use intrapersonal intelligence to react as World War I soldiers.
- Students "learn through their muscles" to empathize with the physical discomforts of trench warfare.
- Only ten minutes are required to transform your classroom into a World War I battlefield.

Student recreate life in a trench during World War I as they view slides of the Western Front and listen to excerpts from All Quiet on the Western Front.

Dress for Success

The day before your students will be sitting in "trenches," tell them to wear clothes appropriate for sitting on the floor.

CHAPTER 4

Strategy Four: Problem-Solving Groupwork

During Problem-Solving Groupwork tasks, students sit in heterogeneously mixed groups to work on challenging projects, such as preparing a dramatization of some aspect of history or drawing a visual metaphor to represent a historical period. The projects require the use of multiple abilities so that every student can contribute. Each student is given a defined role—such as graphic designer, stage manager, director, or script writer. As students work on the task, the teacher serves as a resource. After completing the task, groups present their findings to the class.

Debra Schneider, who teaches middle school social studies, began using cooperative groupwork during her first week of teaching. Both her teacher-education courses and her district's staff-development program emphasized the use of cooperative groupwork as championed by such nationally known researchers as Spencer Kagan, Robert Slavin, and David Johnson. Debra divided her students into heterogeneous groups, gave them challenging tasks, assigned roles, promoted positive interdependence, and allowed for both group and individual accountability.

Cooperative learning seemed to work fine the first year, but by the second year Debra was experiencing some doubts about the technique. In one of her seventh-grade classes, it appeared that some students considered themselves higher-level learners and treated other students as lower-level learners. For example, Jane dominated the interaction in her group, constantly argued with group members, and made negative remarks about other students. Moving Jane to other groups didn't solve the problem, and Debra was eventually forced to remove her from groupwork entirely. "It was horrible," Debra says. "I went from winning an award as an outstanding first-year teacher to a second year in which I couldn't make cooperative learning work effectively for my students."

History Alive!

"They remembered details about the Crusades all year long."
Debra Schneider

Debra's principal introduced her to the research findings of Elizabeth Cohen from the Stanford University School of Education. Cohen and her associates have discovered that when students work together on a collective task, an unequal status order emerges. High-status students tend to dominate group interaction, leaving their low-status peers out of the loop. As a result of their increased interaction, high-status students learn more. Debra realized she had a status problem in her classroom, but didn't know how could she equitably involve all her students in the groupwork process.

The key to overcoming status problems during groupwork, according to Cohen, is to create an academic task that requires the use of a wide range of abilities—linguistic, artistic, interpersonal, spatial, kinesthetic—and telling students: No one will be good at all of these abilities. But everyone will be good with at least one.

Debra decided to try the technique. She created a multiple-ability groupwork task revolving around the Crusades. Each group was to create a multimedia presentation about some group affected by the Crusades, such as Byzantine Jews, European Christians, peasants, or Muslims. Debra explained that the task would require a range of abilities and that every group member would have something of value to contribute. As students prepared their presentations, Debra observed that the high-status students no longer dominated and that the students worked together more equitably.

"Students presented choreographed sword fights with intricate commentary and television programs complete with clever commercials," Debra says. "After each presentation we were able to have a substantial class discussion about some aspect of the Crusades in which students used higher-order thinking skills. They remembered details about the Crusades all year long."

The Promise and Peril of Cooperative Groupwork

Social studies educators and researchers have long advocated the use of cooperative groupwork. Despite their best attempts to make groupwork run smoothly, however, teachers often report that the strategy results in unequal and ineffective student interaction—the very outcomes most advocates hoped to overcome. Teachers typically report that some students dominate the process, while others leave the driving to the domineering students. One frustrated teacher asks, "How do I prevent one person from taking over the group while another person sits back and says very little?"

Cohen believes the problem of unbalanced student interaction stems from status differences—differences in how the students rank each other on academic abilities and differences in personal standing and popularity. Group members who have a high rank are seen as more competent and are generally expected to do well. These high-status students are likely to command their groups; many students defer to these "stars" because they view them as more competent. Other group members are seen as less competent and are expected to do less well. These low-status students withdraw, distract others, and sometimes misbehave because they know they are not expected to contribute anything valuable. Those who do not participate because they are low status learn less; high-status students learn more because they interact more.

Cohen and her associates have discovered that a multiple-ability approach to cooperative learning can overcome the problem of unequal status inter-

Chapter 4

action and lead to higher learning gains for all students.[1] Much of what she advocates—carefully preparing students to work together, designing high-level groupwork tasks, dividing the class into heterogeneous groups, giving each student a role, and allowing the groups to resolve their own problems without unnecessary teacher intervention—is standard practice among cooperative learning advocates such as Slavin, Johnson, and Kagan. What sets her apart from other researchers, however, is her insistence that teachers deal with status inequities by creating multiple-ability groupwork tasks that allow students with a variety of learning styles to interact with each other during the groupwork process.

Cooperative groupwork can be an effective strategy for improving interaction and learning among students if one of the greatest barriers to cooperation—unequal status interaction—is acknowledged and a few simple, powerful steps are taken to ensure effective learning. The rest of this chapter details the steps you can take to create multiple-ability Problem-Solving Groupwork activities.

Preparing Students for Cooperation

Before students undertake their first Problem-Solving Groupwork task, you must prepare them to work together in small groups. Many students have had few successful experiences in cooperative tasks—in school, at home, or among their friends. Students must be prepared for cooperation so they know how to behave in the group without direct supervision.

Train students to work together cooperatively so they become responsible for their own behavior and learning.

How Much Groupwork?

Curriculum developers should find ways of infusing cooperative, multiple-ability groupwork tasks into on-going courses. Each teaching unit in a semester- or year-long course might include one or two groupwork

"Traditional classroom norms—do you own work and don't pay attention to what other students are doing, never give or ask for advice from a fellow student while doing an assignment in class, pay attention to what the teacher is saying and doing and not to anything else, eyes front and be quiet—reinforce competitiveness and do not give students the skills they need to work effectively together."[2]

Elizabeth Cohen

History Alive!

> *"Perhaps the most important outcomes of these cooperative experiences are in the affective domain, for example, mutual concern, friendships with students of other races, liking school, and perceiving peer support."*[3]
> **Jane Stallings and Deborah Stipek,**
> *Educational Researchers*

Set aside class time to create a new set of cooperative norms, as discussed in Chapter 7. Those ten practical steps will help you replace the traditional norms students have internalized over the years. One cooperative norm is that everyone has the right to ask for help and the duty to assist anyone that asks for help. Other useful cooperative norms include knowing and using names, making eye contact with other group members, and listening closely to what others say.

While these norms can be applied during any activity, they are an imperative for groupwork. Students will learn to depend on each other. They will learn to ask for and receive help. They will learn to respect the ideas and values of everyone in the classroom, including you. And, more specifically, they will learn concrete behaviors that will help them succeed during groupwork tasks. Teaching your students these norms for cooperative, tolerant interaction is one of the most lasting gifts you can give them: a self-management system students can benefit from when they interact in the future with employers, colleagues, and family members.

Brainstorming Ideas for Engaging, Challenging Groupwork

Successful groupwork tasks challenge students to use their problem-solving skills to find innovative answers to complex problems, such as creating a dramatic presentation about some aspect of history, bringing the ideas of a historical figure to life, or creating a visual metaphor representing a period of history. Nothing kills the enthusiasm and meaningful interaction of a small group faster than working on a simple task with discrete answers, such as labeling physiographic landmarks on a map or plotting the points of a line graph. You simply don't need four or five heads to figure out answers to simple questions. If you give small groups limited tasks, be prepared for limited engagement and complaints about "boring" group projects. You do need four or five people, however, to tackle open-ended questions with no "right" answers. Your tasks should be challenging and engaging enough to warrant the collective genius of several students and inspire them to use their best critical-thinking skills.

> *"We only think when we are confronted with a problem."*
> **John Dewey**

> *"Too often we give students answers to remember rather than problems to solve."*
> **Roger Lewin**

After you choose a possible task for a groupwork assignment, ask yourself these five questions (from the work of Dr. Rachel Lotan, Stanford University).

1. Does the task require multiple abilities?
2. Does the task have more than one answer or more than one way to solve the problem?
3. Does the task challenge students to use their problem-solving skills?
4. Does the task allow for multiple perspectives?
5. Will the task be challenging enough to create initial frustration, yet give students a sense of accomplishment once they complete it?

If you can answer yes to all of these questions, chances are you have picked an appropriate task and are well on your way to creating engaging and challenging Problem-Solving Groupwork activities. Let's analyze how two successful groupwork projects challenged students to use their problem-solving skills.

☐ Creating Metaphors of U.S. Foreign Policy

In a Problem-Solving Groupwork task examining the growth of U.S. imperialism at the turn of the century, students were challenged to think metaphorically about the motives behind expansionism and the reactions of those being influenced by the Americans. Each group explored and completed a project on the involvement of the United States in one of the following territories: Cuba, the Philippines, Hawaii, Panama, China, the Dominican Republic, and Puerto Rico. Each group created two metaphors with illustrations, one showing how the U.S. government saw its role in the territory and the other showing how the territory saw the U.S. role in its own region. Students drew or painted the metaphors on poster board; each metaphor used one half of the board and had a title reading: "From the perspective of (name of territory), U.S. foreign policy was like (choice of metaphor)." Underneath each title, students created a bold, artistic image of the metaphor. Alongside the image, they placed the word "because" followed by three reasons the metaphor accurately described U.S. foreign policy.

This task successfully engaged students' problem-solving skills because of its open-ended nature. Students created a wonderful variety of metaphors, such as Uncle Sam as the police officer of the world, the United States as a blood-thirsty octopus strangling its territories, and the United States as a wise and patient father overseeing the democratic development of its unruly territories. The activity allowed students to consider U.S. imperialism from multiple perspectives, challenged them to create an interesting visual product, gave students with many different interests something to contribute, and left them with a sense of accomplishment.

☐ Multimedia Presentations on Life in the 1920s

In this Problem-Solving Groupwork activity, students created multimedia presentations representing one of six key areas of change in 1920s society: prohibition, sports, consumer habits, the role of women, the advent of motion pictures, and new forms of transportation. Students were told that in a decade more familiar with the mores of the Victorian age, the changing social attitudes of the 1920s caused tensions between the young and the old, the urban and the rural, the poor and the rich. Students were challenged to create multimedia presentations—combining written resources, slides, music, and video—that presented a social change and the resulting tensions. They were to compare those tensions with similar tensions in today's society.

This activity appealed to the interest students have in the media and social history. The result was animated group interaction during which students, often those not motivated by traditional academic tasks, became involved in planning musical selections, creating visuals, and selecting video clips. One group of students used music from the 1920s as a background for commercials advertising products of the 1920s and video clips to show how music is used today to hock comparable products. Another group compared photographs of methods used to evade prohibition to photographs depicting problems with drug use in America today. The presentations created heated classroom discussions during which students used their critical-thinking skills to answer such questions as: Why does change cause tension? Was the magnitude of social change in the 1920s greater or less than changes we are experiencing today?

"At first the high-academic kids didn't think these activities were bookish enough. But they began really cooperating and helping each other. I think it's valuable for them to realize that other people learn differently and have other talents."
Jim Kentris,
High School Teacher

"Genuine understanding is most likely to emerge, and be apparent to others, if people possess a number of ways of representing knowledge of a concept or skill and can move readily back and forth among these forms of knowing. No one person can be expected to have all modes available, but everyone ought to have available at least a few ways of representing the relevant concept or skill."[5]
Howard Gardner

History Alive!

Designing Groupwork Tasks with Multiple Abilities in Mind

Once you have thought of a task you feel will fully engage students' problem-solving skills, make sure it also requires the use of multiple abilities so that all students will have something to contribute. A powerful tool to keep in mind while developing multiple-ability groupwork tasks is Howard Gardner's list of seven intelligences: linguistic, logical-mathematical, body-kinesthetic, visual-spatial, musical-rhythmic, intrapersonal, and interpersonal.[4]

Let's analyze how a groupwork task about the Nez Percé taps into Gardner's intelligences. In this activity, students analyze and interpret lyrics from Fred Small's song "Heart of the Appaloosa." This song chronicles the historic retreat of the Nez Percé from the U.S. Cavalry in the late 1800s and serves as a case study for the larger issue of Native-American removal during the nation's greatest territorial expansion.

After a brief lecture about the background of the Nez Percé, students listen to the song, then divide into groups and receive lyrics to one of the nine verses. The lyrics are accompanied by primary and secondary sources that include geographic, historical, and cultural information. Groups interpret their lyrics and create a short presentation to share their interpretation with the class. Each group shows a slide of the Nez Percé, chosen from a group of slides taken from a variety of books, and relates it to ideas, values, and feelings associated with the Nez Percé and their displacement. In addition, each group creates a visual representation—a poster, collage, symbolic drawing, or illustration. The group decides how to integrate the slide, the visual representation, the playing of their verse, and their interpretation of the lyrics into the presentation. This groupwork task challenges students to use a range of abilities, such as

- the linguistic ability to read resource documents, write a script, and make an oral presentation
- the logical ability to determine how the resource documents connect with the song and how best to present the information
- the visual ability to analyze slides of the Nez Percé, draw visual representations, and decide how to use various media to create an effective presentation
- the musical ability to interpret the song and derive meaning from the music
- the kinesthetic ability to use body movements to explain ideas
- the intrapersonal ability to empathize with the plight of the Nez Percé, connect the past with their own lives, and have the self-confidence to give a presentation
- the interpersonal ability to work with one another to complete a complex task

"To do the work right, you have to have the ideas of everyone, not just one person. It takes everyone to make it work."
Middle School Student

Chapter 4

A Word About Choosing Resources for Groupwork Projects

As you brainstorm ideas for engaging, multiple-ability groupwork tasks, be aware of the resources available to you. You can have the most exciting idea in the world, but without adequate resources, it will end up as *just* an idea. Before you get too far in planning a groupwork project, identify a rich collection of resources for students to use during the activity. Some teachers *begin* with a particular assortment of resources—a group of beautiful historic images, a moving song with detailed lyrics, a collection of gripping historic biographies, a series of outstanding maps—that inspires them to create successful groupwork projects.

Once you have an idea for a project and have identified some excellent resources, the challenge is to make those resources useful and accessible to students. Here are three examples of Problem-Solving Groupwork activities that illustrate how teachers turned readily available resources and into suitable materials for their students.

☐ Creating Minidramas on Life During the Great Depression

In this Problem-Solving Groupwork activity, students created a dramatic presentation that brings to life the experience of one social group—families,

Photographs, such as this one taken by Dorthea Lange during the Great Depression, give students a dramatic visual around which to create a minidrama showing what happened before, during, and after the photograph was taken.

> *"I never do a groupwork project until I have found some really great resources. Otherwise, the activities take too long to create and students may not have enough information to successfully complete them."*
> **Mary Smathers,**
> **High School Teacher**

> *"Feudal minidramas helped me learn a lot about how people in the Middle Ages lived. It was easier to learn by doing this because instead of only reading about the people, we read and acted out what their life was about."*
> **Middle School Student**

History Alive!

women, children, businessmen, African Americans, laborers, farmers, or Mexican Americans—during the Great Depression. The dramatic Depression-era photographs of Dorthea Lange and other government-sponsored photographers served as an excellent resource around which to build this activity. The teacher selected one action-filled photograph for each social group to give students plenty of visual clues to create a minidrama depicting what happened before, during, and after the photograph was taken.

The teacher made the photographs into placards, for groups to use in the planing process, and into slides, to be projected onto a large wall and serve as a backdrop for the presentations. In addition to dramatic photographs, the teacher used primary source quotes from Stud Terkel's *Hard Times* and literary quotes from John Steinbeck's *The Grapes of Wrath*. The resulting presentations were dramatic and focused, and led to a rich discussion about the human impact of the Great Depression.

☐ A Press Conference on the Eve of the Civil War

This Problem-Solving Groupwork activity helped students explore various viewpoints on the crisis facing the North and the South after Fort Sumnter was fired upon in 1861. The teacher wanted his students to appreciate the complexity and volatility of the causes of the Civil War from a variety of perspectives. He had located a resource that included well-written biographies of nine key Civil-War-era personalities—Abraham Lincoln, Horace Greeley, Frederick Douglass, Ann Ella Carroll, Henry Clay, Robert E. Lee, John C. Calhoun, Jefferson Davis, and Clement Vallandigham—and a photograph or drawing of each person. He decided to create a fictitious press conference in which each group would prepare an actor to take on the role of one of the nine characters. His well-selected resource made this a fairly simple task.

He prepared the student materials by enlarging each biography on a photocopying machine, cutting out irrelevant sections, and pasting the remaining sections onto a handout in short, readable passages. Each passage was followed by a series of discussion questions. As students read the handout, they discussed details about that person's life and opinions, helping to prepare the actor for his or her upcoming role. The teacher also enlarged the likenesses of each historical personality to life-size. This final photocopy was copied onto heavy paper and turned into a realistic mask for the actor to wear during the press conference.

This activity did not take an exorbitant amount of time to develop, but led to a lively class presentation. The student actors were well prepared to represent and bring their personality to life.

☐ In Touch with the Land: Envisioning Native-American Cultures

A U.S. history teacher began her course with a groupwork activity that challenged her students to speculate and discover how Native Americans adapted to the land. She was initially skeptical about finding geographic information on different areas in North America, and even more skeptical about finding images of Native Americans living on the land before the arrival of Europeans. So, before investing much time in the project, she set out to find the necessary resources.

"It is not enough to create a rich multiple abilities task—in addition, the teacher must be able to describe the particular abilities required by the task. If you fail to do this, students will assume there is only one ability necessary for successful performance."[6]

Elizabeth Cohen

Bios Made Easy

To create historical biographies for press conferences quickly, use readily available secondary sources: encyclopedias, textbooks, and biographical anthologies.

Chapter 4

Edward Curtis captured powerful images of Native Americans in their pristine environments, such as this one of a group of Piegan horsemen surveying a river valley. Rich groupwork tasks can be designed around such excellent resources.

She selected eight geographical regions in North America—Northwest Coast, Great Basin, Plateau, Southwest, California, Great Plains, Eastern Woodlands, and Southeast— for which she had already found ample descriptive information in reference books. She summarized the information on a student handout by dividing it into simple categories: physical features, climate, water availability, animal life, and vegetation. She wanted her students to read the information and hypothesize about the housing, clothing, food, recreation, and values of the Native Americans there. She also wanted each group to learn about a Native-American tribe that had adapted to a particular region. Fortunately, she found several books filled with the wonderful photographs by Edward Curtis of Native Americans in their pristine environments before the mass arrival of Europeans in the late 1800s. These photographs and accompanying descriptions of Native-American lifestyles gave each group the information it needed to create detailed and historically accurate presentations.

Assigning Roles

After you have divided students into heterogeneous groups (as described in Chapter 7), one of the most efficient methods for creating smooth-functioning and productive groups is to give each student a specific role to perform—such as graphic designer, actor, stage manager, or director—and to give the group clear instructions on how to proceed. This will help ensure that all students contribute and will help prevent one member from

The Need for Interdependent Roles

Assigning students meaningful roles guarantees that each student in the group will have some way to help the group. The key to creating these roles is to make them interdependent—each student must rely on the others in the group to complete the project successfully.

History Alive!

dominating the group process. The key to creating these roles is to find an efficient division of labor so that each student is doing part of the groupwork task, but that all parts of the task are positively interdependent. Each student will have a personal sense of accomplishment, and the group cannot produce a successful presentation without the cooperation of all of its members.

Creating Effective Roles

An example of how roles were used effectively during a groupwork task can be seen in an activity a U.S. history teacher developed on the U.S. Constitution. Each group was asked to create an appropriate visual metaphor to complete this statement: "The three branches of government under the Constitution are like a. . . . " Groups either chose one of five metaphors provided for them—a three-ring circus, a football team, a musical band, a tricycle, or a three-part machine—or developed one of their own. They used poster board and butcher paper to create a visual representation of their metaphor, complete with title, illustrations, and explanations of key similarities and differences between the metaphor and the three branches of government. Here is an explanation of the student roles, along with instructions for the activity, which could be made into a student handout or projected as an overhead transparency:

1. Give each group four copies of a student handout outlining guidelines for creating a metaphor, a piece of poster board or butcher paper, and colored pens, crayons, or colored pencils.
2. Make sure everybody understands his or her role:

   Project Manager. Assures the metaphor project is complete, accurate, and creative. Leads the brainstorming session and gives everyone an equal chance to contribute ideas for the metaphor. Works closely with the Presenter to determine ways to incorporate the required components into the metaphor. Sees that all required components are included on the poster.

   Presenter. Presents the group's metaphor to the class. Points out the similarities and differences between the illustrated idea and the three branches of government. Contributes ideas for the metaphor. Works closely with the Project Manager to determine ways to incorporate the required components into the metaphor.

   Graphic Designer. Responsible for creating the "look" for the poster. Takes notes and contributes ideas during the brainstorming session. Determines what kinds of visuals should be incorporated in the poster. Works closely with the Artist to create a rough sketch of the poster. Assists the Artist with the final production.

   Artist. Has primary responsibility for creating the artwork for the poster. Contributes ideas during the brainstorming session. Works with the Graphic Designer to create both the rough draft and final draft. Participates in the group brainstorming session, contributing ideas for the different visuals. Holds the poster during the presentation.

3. Review the student handout carefully. Choose the best metaphor. Brainstorm ideas for how to label and explain the visual metaphor in the most accurate way. Make sure you have all the necessary features on the poster.
4. Have Artist and Graphic Designer create a rough sketch of the poster. Have all group members give suggestions for improvements.
5. Complete the final draft of the poster. Help prepare the Presenter for the presentation.

Note that in this project there is a clear division of labor: each role has a name and a list of expected behaviors. But group members cannot sit apart from the group to complete their job; the roles also provide for positive interdependence. Also note that students are given clear instructions on how to proceed. Clear and concise instructions are essential to smooth-running groupwork. Continue to project the instructions as groups work. If a group has a question about procedures, you can refer them to the instructions and challenge them to answer their own question.

Further Questions About the Groupwork Process

If you create well-defined roles and give clear instructions, you will be well on your way to experiencing success with this strategy. After one or two groupwork activities, however, most teachers have several additional questions about groupwork. Here are some questions and answers generated by teachers who have used groupwork.

How long do I keep my students in the same group? Many teachers put students in a group for one activity and then switch them for the next project. But reassigning students to groups for every project is time consuming; you need to spend time forming the groups, and you need to give students time to team-build in their new groups. On the other hand, many cooperative-learning experts advocate keeping students in the same groups for the entire semester or even the entire year. But this does not allow them to build social skills with other class members, and it doesn't provide you with the opportunity to disband the occasional dysfunctional group. Many teachers have found that keeping students in the same group for two or three projects is most effective.

Do I assign students only to roles I know they will be strong at? The purpose of assigning roles is to give every student the opportunity to contribute and to learn through experience how to work with others. If you assign students only to roles they are comfortable in, you will limit the learning experience. Each role has a unique lesson. So give the role of facilitator, for example, not only to the natural leader, but to others as well; all students can benefit from taking a leadership role, especially when they are likely to experience success because you have set clear expectations and created a supportive environment.

There is one situation, however, in which assigning students to a role at which you know he or she will excel is desirable. The first time you do a groupwork project that calls for an unusual presentation or product, give key roles to strong students so that most groups experience success. For

"As the students worked on the Constitutional metaphor project, I was struck by how well all group members contributed to the completion of the project."
**David Ellison,
Middle School Teacher**

"Problem-solving groupwork is quite fun. I like acting out things, making minidramas, and working on real court cases. I didn't realize how much you can learn this way that can help you in real life."
Middle School Student

"Usually I do not like groupwork, but I felt as if these exercises used a lot of my abilities and were more organized and concise."
High School Student

History Alive!

example, the first time students prepare to recreate a historic press conference, the role of actor should go to students who are self-confident in front of others. The first time students are asked to create visual metaphors, the role of artist should go to a student with strong artistic ability.

What do I do about groups that don't work well together? Once standards for cooperative interaction have been established (see Chapter 7), most groups will work together smoothly. However, some conflict between group members is inevitable and should not be taken as a sign of failure or as an opportunity for you to intervene and solve the problem. Rather, view the conflict as a learning opportunity. Ask the group, What seems to be the difficulty? and have them think of strategies for handling the conflict. Most students can develop workable strategies for managing conflict if you challenge them to do so. If the problem is due to a particularly volatile combination of students, however, make a note not to put that combination together again. Changing the composition of groups on a regular basis and rotating roles will help defuse interpersonal problems so that the conflict does not become chronic.

What if the conflict is caused by just one student? If the problem seems to be created by a particularly difficult student, observe that student closely. Exactly how is he or she behaving? How does the group respond? What interests, needs, and strengths does the student exhibits? Take the student aside and share your observations in an nonjudgmental, nonpunitive discussion. Ask the student: Are my observations correct? Is there a reason you are behaving this way? What could you do to make things run smoother? What could the group do? What could I do? You will usually discover that the student is experiencing interpersonal conflict not only in the group, but with friends or family as well. Taking time to listen will probably make the student feel more comfortable in your class and willing to work on changing behavior. Tell the student you have created a class environment where he or she will be safe and supported in making these changes. But then set some clear expectations for future behavior, and remind the student that you are assigning individual as well as group grades for each groupwork assignment. Include the possibility that if the conflict continues, you will remove the student from groupwork altogether.

What happens when students are absent in the middle of groupwork projects? Several techniques will minimize the inconvenience of absent group members. Tell students in advance that, at any time, they may need to take on an additional role. Have students leave all group materials (scripts, visuals, notes, costumes, masks) in the classroom so that the group process does not come to a halt if a student is at home with key resources. Encourage students to exchange phone numbers so they can keep each other informed if they are going to be absent. Make sure students understand that part of their grade depends on their participation in groupwork projects so that they are fully aware of the consequences of being absent. Have an alternative assignment prepared for those students who are absent for the majority of an activity.

Create a Sense of Urgency

Some Problem-Solving Groupwork tasks may take only a single period; others may require several periods. To make sure your students use their time wisely, you might initially tell them that they will have a shorter time to complete the project than you think they actually need. You can always tell them later that they have an additional class period to complete the task if "they make an extra effort to create a really great product."

"These activities are like real life, and they are a challenge."
Middle School Student

How often should I assign Problem-Solving Groupwork projects? Assign enough of these activities during the year so that students learn how to work in groups, but not so often that students become bored with the strategy. Teachers typically assign between eight to ten groupwork tasks a year and find that students benefit from repeating certain types of tasks, such as minidramas or interview panels, as many as three times. This helps them build on their successes and gives them greater confidence. Ultimately, you are the best judge of when and how many times to use Problem-Solving Groupwork before it loses its effectiveness.

Your Role During the Groupwork Process

Assigning students to work in small groups dramatically changes your role. No longer are you a direct supervisor of students, responsible for insuring that they complete their tasks exactly as instructed. No longer is it your responsibility to make sure everything that is said about history is accurate by correcting it on the spot. Instead, you delegate authority to groups of students. They are empowered to make mistakes, to assess their errors, and to discover ways of correcting the situation.

This does not mean that you relinquish your authority. On the contrary, it is your job to develop multiple-ability tasks, to divide students into groups, to assign roles, and to hold groups responsible for creating high-quality products. There are several ways to facilitate the groupwork process in your new role as a supportive supervisor.

■ **Challenge the group to figure out procedures on their own.** At the beginning stages of a groupwork project, it is common for students to ask questions about procedures. Most are answered by the task instructions. Tell students to study the instructions and see if they can discover answers to their questions. Many teachers allow only the facilitator to approach the instructor with questions, further specifying that this is not to take place until the group is sure that no one knows the answer. Some only accept team questions, those in which all group members have their hands in the air.

■ **Observe students carefully from a discrete distance.** Show that you are interested in the groupwork process by moving about the classroom and discretely listening in on groups. If you sit behind your desk and busy yourself with another project, students may infer that you do not value their efforts at working together and, as a result, may tend to socialize or tune out during groupwork tasks. Carefully observing your students will also provide you with the information you might need to help a group that becomes stuck.

■ **Ask key questions of groups that are not making progress.** If a group gets stuck, you may want to ask a few open-ended questions to redirect the group discussion. Suggest that the group deal with your questions on their own, but before you walk off, tell them that you will check with them in fifteen or twenty minutes to find out how they resolved a particular problem.

■ **Challenge students to remember specific cooperative norms.** If a group appears not to be practicing a particular cooperative norm—for example, sharing materials—you might stop for a few moments and ask them which norm they feel is being forgotten. If necessary, post a list of cooperative skills

"Allowing my students to work in groups on projects changed my self-conception as a teacher. No longer was I the sage on the stage, rather I became the guide on the side. Everyone benefited."
Bob Ruark,
Middle School Teacher

Your role during the groupwork process is to let go and allow students to work.

History Alive!

(see Chapter 7) as a reminder. Challenge students to have a brief discussion among themselves to figure out which cooperative norm they forgot to practice and how they might put that norm into action to help the group run more smoothly.

- **Help groups locate additional resources.** Plan ahead. If a group comes to you with a request for further materials, try to have other books, magazines, newspapers, art supplies, musical selections, or other resources available. If you cannot have additional resources in the classroom, prepare the school librarian to handle your students' needs.

- **Praise groups for solving difficult questions.** If you observe that a group, after considerable trial and error, has solved a difficult problem, take a moment to specifically recognize that achievement. Nothing encourages students more than recognizing and praising true accomplishment.

Getting the Most out of Student Presentations

At the end of each Problem-Solving Groupwork project, students share the product they created. That product might be a colonial brochure advertising the features of a particular colony, a minidrama bringing to life some scene from medieval life in China, or a newscast about the effect of World War II on some group of Americans. Presentations must be as clear and informative as possible because this is usually the only time the historical information will be presented to the entire class. While students generally remember the key information their group focused on—say the effect of World War II on Japanese-Americans—they tend not to remember much about other groups' topics—such as the effect of World War II on women, consumers, African Americans, or Mexican Americans—unless those groups give memorable presentations. Here are steps you can take to make sure your students give high-quality presentations.

1. Set high expectations for presentations. Tell your students that you have heard (you heard it right here) about other students who made a similar presentation that was truly outstanding. If your students are to present a panel discussion, for example, tell them that another group of students used elaborate props, accents, quotes from historic personalities, and great costumes. If necessary, give your students an extra period of groupwork time "to really prepare for a spectacular presentation."

2. Rearrange your classroom for dramatic, intimate presentations Most classroom arrangements are awkward and uncomfortable for presentations; there is little room in front for the presenters to maneuver, and desks stretch to the back of the classroom in long rows, making it difficult for many in the audience to see or hear. Clear a stage area in the front of the classroom, and ask students to arrange their desks into a crescent shape surrounding it. This theater-in-the-round arrangement focuses student attention on the presentation and makes for a more intimate exchange between audience and performers.

3. Use props and stage lighting to reduce tension. Think of ways students can use props—masks, posters, costumes, physical objects—not only to make their presentations more dramatic, but also to put themselves more at ease.

Throw Your Early Birds Another Worm

Help groups that finish early to continue refining and improving their product. If a group has finished its project early, you might open up the task once more by asking further questions or challenging the group to improve or expand on the product they just created.

"I get a kick out of watching groups present their products to the class. The pride some of them take in what they have produced is remarkable. Some students beam during their presentations."
Mary Smathers,
High School Teacher

Most students are shy about performing in a bright classroom; they prefer the safety of a darkened room where they can concentrate more on their performance than on the reaction of their peers. If you were to ask students to form into "human statues" representing daily life in Constantinople, for example, allow them to get into position beneath a large sheet, and then dramatically unveil the statue. This technique makes students less self-conscious and allows them to move into unusual and effective formations. Turning off all the lights in the classroom (except for the light from a projected slide or an overhead transparency) has a similar liberating effect on performance during dramatic presentations.

4. Create a clear handout for students to record what they see and hear. To help students remember the salient points of each presentation, provide them with a handout on which to record basic notes. You might provide a matrix that allows students to record similar information about each presentation so they can compare all the ideas after the last presentation. For example, as each group presents a minidrama on medieval life in Europe, the rest of the class takes notes on a matrix with four labeled columns: What is the topic of this minidrama? What happened in the minidrama? What did it teach you about feudal life? Compare the minidrama to life today.

5. Debrief each presentation for deeper meaning and historical accuracy. After each presentation, ask the group some probing questions to further reveal historical information. This is also an appropriate time to point out any historical inaccuracies students presented. For example, during a panel discussion about the Progressive period, one actor portrayed Teddy Roosevelt as a quiet, unassuming person. It was important for the teacher to explain that, while the words spoken by the actor reflected historic reality, his demeanor did not. Similarly, during a minidrama on life in the Depression, students portrayed a group of people waiting in a bread line as indignant and aggressive. The teacher pointed out, however, that during the Depression Americans felt great shame at taking government "handouts." Students are eager to know how accurately they portrayed history and appreciate your historical comments.

6. Prepare a list of critical-thinking questions for a class discussion after the last presentation. After the final group presents, be prepared to hold a class discussion that ties together everything students saw and heard. A few well-chosen questions will challenge your students to use critical-thinking skills. For example, after groups present three-minute advertisements to sell some aspect of ideology from the United States or the former Soviet Union to the rest of the world—such as capitalism, socialism, freedom, equality, individualism, collectivism, democracy, or totalitarianism—you might ask the following questions:

- What are the advantages and disadvantages of both systems?
- Which American value do you most cherish? Which Soviet value do you wish American society would adopt?
- What are the connections between Soviet values of equality, collectivism, socialism, and totalitarianism?

Rearrange your classroom for dramatic, intimate presentations, such as this minidrama about Medieval Europe.

"Watching my friends present what their groups did is fun and it's better than just listening to the teacher talk."
Middle School Student

Overcoming Performance Anxiety

Acknowledge that class members may be feeling anxious about performing in front of their peers, and ask the rest of the students to be particularly attentive and supportive. As the first group assembles for its presentation, give a warm introduction and lead the class in a round of applause.

History Alive!

- What are the connections between the American values of freedom, individualism, capitalism, and democracy?
- What problems were created when these contrasting systems represented the ideologies of the two greatest superpowers?

Evaluating Groupwork Activities

Grading Problem-Solving Groupwork activities raises many questions: Should group evaluation be determined by excellence of the final product or the process used to create it? Should each student in a group receive the same grade? How do you create individual accountability within a group? What do you do about the student who does very little but whose group does excellent work? What do you do about the outstanding student in a group whose group does only mediocre work? How do you keep track of the goings-on in all the groups so that you can evaluate them fairly? What role, if any, should students have in the evaluative process?

Here are five steps for evaluating Problem-Solving Groupwork activities. They give students a clear understanding of how they will be graded, hold individuals and groups accountable for their work, make the grading process equitable, and allow you to evaluate activities quickly and easily.

1. Set clear criteria for evaluation. Tell students they will be evaluated not only on the how good the group's final product is, but also on how effectively they worked as a team. This underscores the importance of using cooperative skills, as students will know that both product and process will be evaluated.

2. Make individuals and groups accountable. Weight fifty percent of a student's grade on individual contribution and the other fifty percent on the group's performance. Every member gets the same group grade; individual grades differ. In this way, students who do outstanding work in a weak group can still be rewarded—through a superior individual grade—for their efforts. Students who do little but benefit from being in a productive group will not get a good overall grade. Students find this system equitable.

3. Evaluate each group's final product immediately after their presentation. As each presentation unfolds, record your impressions, positive and negative. When it is over and the next group prepares for its presentation, write down your assessment of the first group's product. This information will be helpful when you determine the group grade.

4. Have students complete a Brag Sheet. At the end of a Problem-Solving Groupwork activity, have each student complete a Brag Sheet (see p. 87), or self-assessment, in which they list their own contributions to the group and comment on their group members' performances. This allows students to reflect on the group process and gives you additional information on which to base your evaluation. It also gives students the opportunity to let you know what they did outside of class—library research, meeting with group members on weekends—so that their work gets evaluated fairly. Tell students you will use the information to help you determine a fair grade for the student and their group members. Make clear that Brag Sheets are confidential.

"All real-world performers know the target and the standards, not just their task, in advance."[7]
Grant Wiggins

Grade As They Go

As students are working in groups, circulate around the classroom and observe their behavior. Stand near each group and take notes on how individual students are performing, such as "José is on task and contributing" or "Frannie is doing little to contribute and is engaged in social conversation" or "Mali is sitting quietly but is obviously thinking about the task." This information will be useful when you later determine grades.

Brag Sheet

Name _____

My role in the group was _____

Student Evaluation

List all the ways you helped your group complete this task.

List all the ways you helped your group work effectively and cooperatively.

On a scale of 1 (worst) to 10 (best), I would give my performance on this Problem-Solving Groupwork task a ____ because

On a scale of 1 (did not contribute at all) to 10 (contributed a tremendous amount), I would give each member of my group:

I give _____ a ____ because

I give _____ a ____ because

I give _____ a ____ because

I give _____ a ____ because

Teacher Evaluation

Group Grade   _____

Individual Grade   _____

Overall Grade   _____

Comments   _____

© Addison-Wesley Publishing Company, Inc.

"Before we did Problem-Solving Groupwork, I had one student who was at the bottom of the academic heap. He had failed U.S. history once. But once he began working in his group to create a minidrama, he brought props and watched each visual intently. He got caught up in the enthusiasm. In the end he got one of the highest scores on the test."
Nancy Grippo,
High School Teacher

History Alive!

5. Determine group and individual grades. At this point, you have an abundance of information on which to base grades—your recorded observations both during the groupwork process and immediately after the presentations about the group product, and students' Brag Sheets, which contain a self-assessment and comments on group members' contributions. Use this information to formulate group grades. Remember, the group grade should be based on how well the group worked together (process) and the effectiveness of the presentation (product). Next, formulate individual grades. Consider your observations, the comments made on the Brag Sheets, and other group members' perceptions.

You will notice on the Brag Sheets that students are asked to rate their performance and their group members' performances from 1 (poor) to 10 (outstanding). Use these assessments only as additional pieces of information on which to base your grade; do not add or average them. Again, individual grades should be based on how effectively a student worked in the group and how much he or she contributed to the final product. Record the group and individual grades on each Brag Sheet, total them, write comments below the overall grade, and return the Brag Sheets to the students.

Three Outstanding Problem-Solving Groupwork Activities

☐ Creating Minidramas Illuminating the Impact of the Vietnam War

In this Problem-Solving Groupwork activity, students break into groups of five to study how different individuals were affected by the Vietnam War. Each group of students is assigned a segment of society—African Americans, Vietnamese, Military Opposed, Military in Favor, Politicians Opposed, Politicians in Favor, or Dissenters—to study and portray in a short minidrama that brings a photograph of those people to life. During their presentation they "step into" a slide of the photograph and act out what happened before, during, and after the photograph was taken. They use primary sources, class notes, textbooks, and library resources to discover the essential concerns of the segment of society they are portraying.

Favorite Features

- Student roles require all group members to act in the minidrama.
- This activity requires a variety of skills and abilities: acting, visual, interpersonal, writing, speaking, logical-sequencing, historical interpretation, and the ability to empathize.
- The open-ended nature of this task allows students to create minidramas that are as dramatic as they are poignant.
- This activity capitalizes on students' fascination with the Vietnam War and allows them to study the human aspects of the war in great detail.

Chapter 4

Dramatic photographs, such as this one showing a group of African-American soldiers in Vietnam sitting with Sammy Davis, Jr., can serve as the basis for students to create powerful minidramas.

☐ Creating Monuments to Daily Life in Constantinople

In this Problem-Solving Groupwork activity, students break into groups of four to create monuments commemorating various aspects of daily life in Constantinople. They receive a detailed map of the city and written information on one of nine aspects of daily life during the twelfth century: trade and commerce, housing, religion, public works and charity, education, politics, military protection, recreation, and the treatment of slaves. Each group brainstorms ways to arrange their bodies—set in fixed, frozen positions—and simple props to create a monument that illustrates the aspect of daily life. A group working on recreation, for example, might create a monument with two students positioned as chariot racers and two students as fans cheering them on. Students also create a plaque for their monument, which includes an inscription and symbols, and place it on a detailed map of Constantinople. The monument to recreation, for example, might be located in front of the Hippodrome.

Favorite Features

- Students strong in body-kinesthetic intelligence often find it difficult to understand historical concepts. This activity gives them access to the ideas through physical movement.
- This activity requires students to use their geography skills in combination with spatial and logical intelligence.
- Every group member has a substantive role and responsibility for being part of the monument.

Unveiling Student Masterpieces

Place a sheet over students as they form their monuments, and then remove the sheet to dramatically reveal the statute they have created with their bodies. This allows students to place themselves into unusual positions they might have otherwise felt self-conscious about.

History Alive!

☐ Can Common People Be Trusted to Govern?

This Problem-Solving Groupwork activity allows students to explore the philosophies of government held by nine prominent thinkers—Abigail Adams, Benjamin Banneker, Hiawatha, Thomas Hobbes, King Louis XIV, William Laud, Baron de Montesquieu, Mary Wollstonecraft, and John Locke—and then discuss those philosophies during a "Meet the Press" interview panel that focuses on the question: Can common people be trusted to govern themselves? Each group is given biographical information about one of the thinkers and the task to bring that person to life during a heated question-and-answer panel. When the groups have finished preparing, one student in each group puts on a mask representing the group's thinker and sits in a row in the front of the classroom, facing the rest of the class. The teacher serves as the moderator and is responsible for keeping the discussion lively by pitting the ideas of the historical figures against one another.

These historical masks of figures with disparate views on the proper role of common people in government are worn by students to bring authenticity to a panel discussion.

Favorite Features

- The masks transform the classroom atmosphere and make it seem as if the historical figures are present. Actors often change their voices and use dramatic hand and arm movements to bring their figures to life.
- This activity usually leads to a heated panel discussion that few students want to stop once the debate intensifies.
- The figures on the interview panel represent a range of perspectives on government—from those who believed that the power to govern lay with God to those who believed that people had that power to rule themselves. This helps students understand the complexities of the issue of governance.

Host Your Own Show

Play the part of Oprah Winfrey or Phil Donahue during the interview panel. Dash between panel members and the audience to generate controversy.

CHAPTER 5

Strategy Five: Response Groups

Response Groups enrich class discussion and promote critical thinking. Groups of students receive historical information, view compelling images, read primary sources, or listen to music, and then discuss provocative questions about the material. After the small-group discussions, presenters from each group share findings with the class to stimulate whole-class discussion. Because students have access to rich resources and the ideas of their classmates, response time is far greater than during conventional class discussions.

Diana Ruark, who has taught middle school for almost two decades, is committed to integrating women's issues into her eighth-grade U.S. history classes. To convey the impact and legacy of the Seneca Falls convention, for example, Diana designed a lesson in which students read the Declaration of Sentiments and discussed whether gender equality had been reached today.

"Year after year the discussion was dominated by one or two confident girls who argued that there was still gender discrimination and a handful of boys who said there was not," Diana remembers. "The rest of the class just listened passively and did not participate. Even when I called on other students to draw them into the discussion, I rarely got more than a one-sentence response."

The problem, Diana recognized, was twofold. "The majority of students not only knew too little to answer the question," she says, "but also wouldn't even attempt an answer because they were afraid of peer reaction." Diana became the focal point, providing factual information and her own insights when the discussion lagged. "It became my role to keep the discussion going. A good class discussion should center on students' ideas, not mine."

"The discussion was immediate and animated. Students could hardly wait to share their ideas."

Diana Ruark,
Middle School Teacher

History Alive!

To correct the situation, Diana revamped the lesson by introducing students to five leading women reformers of the nineteenth century: Susan B. Anthony, Elizabeth Cady Stanton, Sojouner Truth, Lucy Stone, and Elizabeth Blackwell. Students viewed a slide of each woman, read biographical information, and listened to a recording of a famous quote. With this preparation, student pairs took the role of each of the reformers to write responses to a sexist quote of the time. This, Diana found, helped students to understand the desire for a women's rights convention and to empathize with women's concerns.

Diana then employed the Response Groups strategy to allow students to critically analyze the Declaration of Sentiments and to discuss gender equality today. Diana placed students into heterogeneous groups of three and projected a slide of the grievance from the Declaration of Sentiments that reads, "He has never permitted her to exercise her inalienable right to the elective franchise. He has compelled her to submit to laws, in the formation of which she had no voice." After Diana made sure everyone understood the grievance, groups were given five to seven minutes to discuss and write answers to the question, To what degree has this grievance been redressed? That is, do women have an equal opportunity to influence political and governmental decision today?

To represent their answers, groups placed a visual marker for politics on a spectrum labeled *Grievance Not Addressed* and *Grievance Fully Addressed* at either end. Students used a two-page fact sheet on women in the United States today and their own experience to guide their discussion.

One student in each group was appointed presenter to facilitate discussion and to share the groups' findings with the class. As groups discussed the grievance, Diana watched in awe. "The discussion was immediate and animated. Students could hardly wait to share their ideas. They were leaning forward, arguing, and moving the symbol back and forth on the spectrum. The amount of interaction was remarkable."

When Diana asked if any presenters would volunteer to share their group's answers, a hand shot up from every group. Presenters confidently articulated their answers because they had both factual information and ideas generated from the group for support.

Diana repeated this process for five other grievances from the Declaration of Sentiments, with the role of presenter rotating within each group. For two class periods, the students—a diverse group of whites, Hispanics, African Americans, and Asians—debated gender issues in America, past and present. "The momentum built as the activity progressed. Presenters respectfully challenged each other's arguments, and students were exposed to a rich array of ideas and beliefs. They were truly excited."

The Benefits of Using Response Groups

In the conventional classroom, class discussion is used after a lecture or reading to foster a deeper understanding of a topic. A handful of students with strong linguistic skills usually dominates discussion, which ends when the teacher hears the answer he or she is looking for. Meanwhile, the majority of students—usually those with weaker linguistic intelligence—listen passively or daydream. Many students simply lack the knowledge, interest, or ability to participate meaningfully in high-level class discussions.

To engage reluctant students, teachers often call on them randomly. The result, in most cases, is predictable: faced with a wave of anxiety as the class awaits their answer, students give abrupt, superficial answers or simply respond, "I don't know."

Response Groups were created to remedy this problem. Putting students in small groups to examine rich resources—images, music, historical biographies, primary and secondary source readings—and discuss corresponding critical-thinking questions enables all students to confidentially share substantive ideas during class discussion. There are several benefits of the strategy.

1. Student interaction greatly increases. There is a strong correlation between interaction and learning. Response Groups activities create high levels of interaction in small groups, which leads to increased learning gains. Small-group discussion on critical-thinking questions provides every student the opportunity to comment and to share ideas. In conventional class discussions, this is virtually impossible.

2. Activities are structured to allow students to answer critical-thinking questions substantively. Students in conventional class discussions are often asked to respond to cold-call questions without the time or background knowledge to answer thoughtfully. During Response Groups activities, students receive the necessary resources—music, images, political cartoons, historical readings, lecture notes—to formulate answers to high-level questions. They also are given time in small groups to discuss, refine, and write their answers before they are required to articulate them to the class.

3. Students use the multiple intelligences. While conventional class discussion is largely a linguistic exercise, Response Groups activities demand the use of multiple intelligences. Discussion is often prompted by group examination of documents such as pictures, political cartoons, drawings, songs, maps, charts, and diagrams, which requires visual-spatial, musical-rhythmic, and logical-mathematical intelligences. Sometimes students use their intrapersonal intelligence to assume the role of a historical figure and articulate a particular point of view. And Response Groups activities always tap into interpersonal intelligence, both when students share ideas in small groups and during the class discussion.

4. Student response time increases dramatically. After having time to examine resources and to discuss critical-thinking questions in small groups, students are prepared to articulate more sophisticated answers. Presenters routinely give responses of thirty to forty-five seconds; some talk much longer. This is a huge increase in response time when compared to conventional class discussions.

5. Discussions focus on students' ideas, not on the teacher's. During conventional class discussions, teachers usually have to coax students into sharing ideas and often end up talking more than the students. Discussion in Response Groups activities centers on the ideas articulated by each group's presenter. Often discussion is so animated that teachers do not have time to hear from all presenters. Teachers become facilitators and rarely have to interject their own ideas into the discussion.

"Before I used this strategy, I had a couple of classes in which class discussion primarily meant a dialogue between a few of my vocal, male students and me. Since I've been using Response Groups, however, all my students get involved. I'm hearing ideas and opinions I never knew existed."
Carmen Gomez,
High School Teacher

Shy No More

Many students are reluctant to share their ideas during conventional class discussions for fear of being wrong or belittled. Remind students that the presenter's answer is, to a large extent, the group's answer. In this way, the onus and risk that each student assumes when responding is limited.

History Alive!

> "In order to learn, students must use what they already know so as to give meaning to what the teacher presents to them."[1]
>
> **National Institute of Education**

Invite Controversy

The more controversial the topic, the more effective Response Groups activities are.

When to Use Response Groups

Response Groups allow students to grapple with the ambiguities of history, to recognize the complexity of historical events, and to discuss the legacies of our past. Discussion is prompted by provocative critical-thinking questions, carefully crafted to spark student interest. This strategy must be employed prudently, however, since class discussion in any form loses its effectiveness when overused. Response Groups activities are most effective when you want students to:

■ **Discuss controversial issues.** History provides numerous controversial issues that motivate students to argue and debate. During a lesson on the impact of the civil-rights movement today, for example, you might prompt students with slides and secondary source materials to discuss such controversial civil-rights issues as busing and affirmative action. During an activity comparing the plight of the homeless with that of medieval serfs, students could view slides of serfs and of homeless people today, listen to quotes from the homeless, and discuss the two situations.

■ **Analyze primary source readings to make historical discoveries.** A key social studies objective is teaching students to read primary source documents to make conclusions about historical events. These readings are often difficult. Putting students in Response Groups will allow them to share ideas. For example, students might compare parts of Justinian's Code of Law from Byzantium to parts of the Penal Code, discussing the relative merits of each and discovering the influence of Justinian's Code on the United States' current legal structure. Or, group members might read and then hear quotes by Alexander Hamilton and Thomas Jefferson and be challenged to use their knowledge to attribute each saying to one of the two.

■ **Solve a historical problem.** Students are motivated to learn about history when they are allowed to solve historical problems. Providing students with the context of a historical dilemma—events leading to the issue, the basis of the problem, possible courses of action—and allowing them to determine a solution gives them a sense of ownership. By becoming involved in the history, students *want* to know what really happened. During an activity about the Cuban missile crisis, for example, students might be placed in a simulation of the tense situation President Kennedy faced in October 1962. Have groups analyze an aerial photo of the missile sites in Cuba and receive information about Cuba's proximity to the United States, the existence of American medium-range missiles in Turkey, and Kennedy's desire to keep missiles out of Cuba. Then present five possible courses of action for Kennedy to take, and have groups rank the relative merits of each. After the class debates what Kennedy should have done, students find out what actually happened. Afterwards, students will be eager to analyze the Kennedy's actions.

■ **Use musical-rhythmic intelligence to help them understand a historical period.** Music can foster a deeper understanding of the attitudes, values, and issues of an era. This often-overlooked resource could be featured, for instance, in a lesson on the changing attitude toward the Civil War. Groups listen to four songs that offer strikingly different views of the Civil War. The first three songs, *Johnny Is My Darling*, *Bonnie Blue Flag*, and *Marching Song of* *the First of Arkansas,* show the similarities and differences in how Northerners, Southerners, and African Americans perceived the war at its outset; the final song, *Tenting Tonight,* provides a soldier's point of view on the brutality and inhumanity of the war. Class discussion centers on how perspective and time affected attitudes toward the war, and how the songs—through music and lyrics—reflected these changes.

■ **Understand multiple perspectives on an event.** To enable students to understand perspective, have groups assume the roles of different historical figures commenting on events of their time. As students discuss historical issues from different points of view, they begin to appreciate the complexity of history. For example, Response Groups could be used to examine various perspectives on colonial rebellion. Each group assumes the role of a historical figure—Samuel Adams, Crispus Attucks, John Dickenson, Abigail Adams, King George III, Thomas Hutchinson, Logan—and examines paintings of the Boston Massacre, the Boston Tea Party, and the tar and feathering of a tax collector. Groups then respond to each of these events in character. A wide array of perspectives on the acts of rebellion are voiced, and students are awakened to the complexity of colonial rebellion.

■ **Use visual literacy skills to make historical discoveries.** Students can make important historical discoveries using visual-spatial intelligence. Pictures, paintings, illustrations, and maps sometimes are the best documents to convey historical concepts. For example, to teach about the family values of middle-class America in the 1950s and early 1960s, you might provide Response Groups with pictures from three popular television shows from the era—say "Hazel," "I Love Lucy," and "Father Knows Best." Groups carefully examine the images to determine what family values were reflected in the shows. This will lead to rich class discussion on the values of the era and allow students to examine the impact of the media in shaping social values today.

Moving Students into Heterogeneous Response Groups

Precise classroom geography is crucial to the success of Response Groups activities. Desks must be arranged so that students in each group can talk among themselves and clearly see the slide screen. The diagrams on pages 96 and 97 illustrate the three important features of the proper classroom arrangement for Response Groups:

1. Each student has a direct view of projected slides *and* the ability to interact with all groups easily.
2. Desks are arrayed along imaginary axes protruding from the center of the slide.
3. A slide can be projected without interference.

"I came in here thinking my views were planted in cement. Now I realize that there is another side. Discussions actually confused my views and made me think."
High School Student

"Because discussion is prompted by slides, role-play, and historic problem solving, kids have a lot to talk about and get to a deeper level of understanding of the history. I don't have superficial discussions just to cover the material anymore."
**Dan Picardi,
High School Teacher**

History Alive!

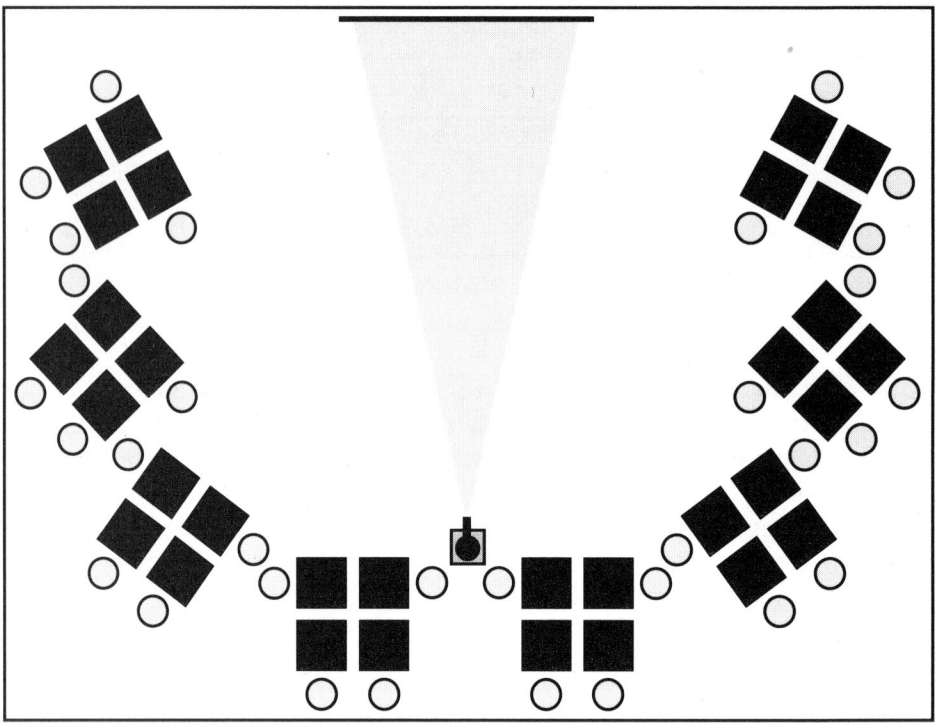

This is a suggested classroom arrangement for four-person Response Groups, often used in high school.

Follow these guidelines to move students efficiently into Response Groups:

■ **Make an overhead transparency of the arrangement.** Create a diagram of the Response Groups classroom arrangement, similar to those shown here. Make heterogeneous groups. List group members' names by each cluster of desks so students know where to sit and who is in their group.

■ **Explain the importance of the arrangement.** Students need to understand the importance of desk arrangement for these activities. Make explicit the goal of the arrangement: to allow all student to see the slide screen and interact with group members at the same time.

■ **Have students practice moving into Response Groups the first time.** Students, even high school students, must be taught how to move into groups, especially into a unique arrangement like this. Chapter 7 (see p. 133) details ways you can accomplish this task.

■ **Do not begin until all groups are arranged precisely.** By waiting to begin a Response Groups activity until all groups are configured to your design, you send a clear message: precise classroom arrangement is important.

Classroom Arrangement: Have Patience

Recognize that effective classroom arrangement for Response Groups—where students can easily talk to one another and see the slide—is difficult for students to set up quickly. Be patient, but expect your students to get it right.

Chapter 5

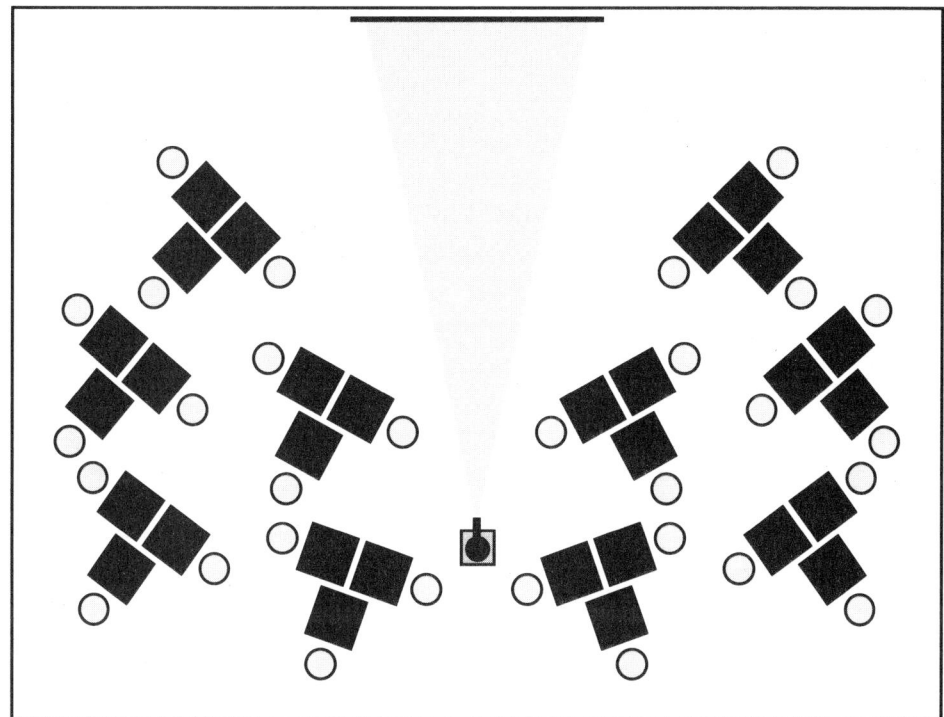

This is a suggested classroom arrangement for three-person Response Groups, often used in middle school. Use a staggered arrangement like this for small classrooms.

Providing the Historical Background for Critical Thinking

To engage in meaningful, high-level discussions, students must have either sufficient background knowledge or rich resources to prompt critical thinking. Jerome Bruner's theory of the spiral curriculum, as discussed in the Introduction, suggests that when students are taught basic concepts first and then progressively more difficult ones, all learners can engage in higher-order thinking. Conventional class discussions often overlook this notion. Teachers might ask high-level questions before most students have the preparatory knowledge to answer them effectively. As a result, these discussions involve only a handful of students.

To ensure success in Response Groups activities, think carefully about how to prepare students to answer critical-thinking questions. Before they can be effective class discussants, students need the "building blocks" of historical knowledge. This preparation comes in two forms: (1) Providing background information via lecture, slide inquiry, or historical reading to allow students to discuss complex historical issues; and (2) Allowing groups to analyze rich historical documents for self-discovery.

Giving Students Historical Information for Critical Thinking

Response Groups activities can be used to discuss controversial issues, to solve historical problems, and to understand multiple perspectives. These tasks require that students have a clear understanding of the topic of discussion.

"I make sure groups don't begin discussion until they feel comfortable with one another. I usually have groups do a team-building activity before they begin discussing."
**Debra Schneider,
Middle School Teacher**

"The discussions in this class are alive. Usually everyone has an opinion and the whole class gets into it."
High School Student

History Alive!

During Response Groups activities, this knowledge must be provided *quickly* so that students can spend the bulk of the activity grappling with critical-thinking questions. Here are three ways to do this.

1. Give a mini-lecture. Often the most expedient way to prepare students for high-level discussion is to lecture, especially for a relatively simple narrative history. In an activity about the relocation of Japanese-Americans during World War II, for example, you might lecture about the rationale for the internment of Japanese-Americans before students, in Response Groups, examine slides and discuss related critical-thinking questions. Mini-lectures must be succinct—no more than five minutes per question—and focus solely on information students need to answer the high-level questions.

2. Provide students with appropriate historical readings. Interesting historical readings can prepare students for discussion and provide them with a reference throughout the activity. This is most effective when students are discussing complex issues and need more substantive resources than lecture notes. In a lesson about the compromises made during the Constitutional Convention, for example, you might give students historical readings that summarize the major conflicts that delegates faced. Students could read and refer to these summaries as groups discuss possible compromises. Without these summary readings, students would lack the requisite understanding to solve the historical problems.

Photographs can provide students with intriguing background information for dynamic class discussions. From this photograph, students could learn about the date, location, and extent of the Soviet military buildup in Cuba.

3. Use compelling slides to create understanding. Powerful images are sometimes more effective than lectures or readings at providing students with background information. With spiral questioning, you can help students discover historical information in such images. During the Response Groups activity on the Cuban missile crisis, for example, you might give students background information by having them examine an image and respond to carefully structured questions. As students see a slide of a U-2 spy plane of Soviet missile sites in Cuba with identifying captions, they might respond to such questions as: What do you see in this picture? When and from where was this picture taken? Who was building the missile sites? Why do you think Soviets wanted sites there? How do you think President Kennedy felt about the construction of sites ninety miles from the Florida coast? After this inquiry process, most students will have the requisite knowledge to discuss critical-thinking questions.

Allowing Students to Discover Information for Critical Thinking

You can design Response Groups activities that will allow students to make historical discoveries, both through small-group and whole-class discussion, for themselves. These types of activities—in which students analyze primary source readings, listen to period music, or examine images to draw conclusions—will not require students to have in-depth background knowledge. Background knowledge would undermine the very discovery process the activities are designed to encourage.

In this type of Response Groups activity, divulge as little information about the topic as possible before discussion begins. Instead, provide students with resources, give brief instructions, and allow them to discuss the insights they gain from the materials. The activity on middle-class values requires students to view slides of scenes from three popular television shows to discover family values of the time. For this activity, simply define the term *value* and give groups time to discover the social values of the era independently.

Designing Provocative Critical-Thinking Questions

Crafting provocative questions is the single most important step in ensuring rich discussion during Response Groups activities. Pose subjective questions that create intellectual tension, invite controversy, and require students to analyze, synthesize, compare, discover, and hypothesize. Here are four methods that prompt critical thinking and energetic discussion.

■ **A single, direct question.** To compare two political cartoons on the New Deal, students might discuss this question: What is the cartoonists' message in each of these political cartoons? To help students discover how New England colonists adapted to their environment, you might show them a detailed drawing of life in a Massachusetts coastal town and have them discuss the question: Based on this picture, in what ways did colonists in New England adapt to the environment?

"I like to sit back and watch groups make historical discoveries on their own. Even though they don't always come up with the right answer, it's fun to watch them develop their deductive thinking skills. And afterwards they really want to know the answer."
Deborah Whitson,
High School Teacher

Students can interpret some photographs without having extensive background information. Students can discuss what this photograph of Doris Day, for example, reveals about middle-class values and the role of women in the 1960s.

"A good question produces a thousand words of discussion."
Patrick McCrystle,
High School Teacher

History Alive!

■ **A series of related questions.** To speculate on the type of dwelling that housed various African tribes during the tenth century, you might have students view slides of different climatic regions and discuss: What resources could Africans use for shelter? Of the resources available, which would make the most durable shelter? What environmental elements—heat, rain, wind, predators—should be considered in building the shelter? What do you think this shelter might look like? To debate the virtue of busing as a means to desegregate schools, students might hear a mini-lecture, view a slide of children on a school bus, and discuss: What are the positive and negative aspects of mandatory school busing? Do you think busing is a good idea? Should the government attempt to desegregate schools today? If so, how? If not, why?

■ **Quantifying an answer on a spectrum.** To consider at the end of a unit whether the United States should be praised or condemned for its actions in the Cold War, students might discuss where to place visual icons of Cold War events—the Vietnam War, the arms race, the Bay of Pigs invasion, the Berlin blockade—on a spectrum between *Totally Praised* and *Totally Condemned*. To argue who was most responsible for the inhumanity of the Holocaust, students might discuss where to place the names of several groups—such as civilian contractors who helped build death camps, members of the S.S., soldiers in the German army, the Catholic Church, collaborators, the U.S. government—on a spectrum from *Most Responsible* to *Least Responsible*.

Providing students with visual icons representing different events and challenging them to place them along a spectrum promotes discussion and shows how exciting—and at times frustrating—multiple perspectives can be.

- **Evaluating possible solutions to historical problems.** To allow middle school students to attempt to resolve the conflict between large states and small states over representation in Congress, students might read a summary of the controversy, examine a map of the United States, and discuss: If you were delegates to the Constitutional Convention, what do you think would be the best way to resolve the problem of representation in Congress? Rank the choices from 1 (best choice) to 4 (worst choice). Then explain your first choice and your last choice.

    A. Have representation in Congress based on population.
    B. Have an equal number of members of Congress from each state.
    C. Create a Congress with two parts. Have representation for one part based on a state's population and representation for the other part based on an equal number of representatives per state.
    D. Redraw the boundaries of the states so that the population is equal in all states. Then base representation in Congress on an equal number of representatives per state.

"I like it when we get to pretend we are government leaders and have come up with ways to deal with some historical event. Groups argue with each other and before you know it the period's over."
High School Student

Discussing Critical-Thinking Questions in Small Groups

Once students have the preparatory knowledge or materials necessary to consider high-level questions, small-group discussion can occur. Small-group discussion gives students the time to discuss, refine, and write answers to critical-thinking questions, and enables all students to confidentially share sophisticated ideas with the whole class after the small-group discussion. Animated, purposeful discussion takes place in small groups when three guidelines are followed.

1. Rotate the role of presenter. At the beginning of a Response Groups activity, assign the role of presenter to one student in each group. Presenters have a twofold responsibility: to act as facilitator during group discussion to make sure all members share their ideas, and to be spokesperson for the group during class discussion. Rotate the role of presenter for each set of critical-thinking questions. Each Response Groups activity should contain four to six topics for discussion, so that each student in the group can be a presenter at least once during the activity.

2. Have each student record answers during group discussion. Give students a handout that lists all critical-thinking questions, and have them write multi-sentence answers for each. Encourage students to embellish their answers as new ideas emerge during class discussion. These requirements allow students to use the writing process to refine their ideas and make students accountable during the entire activity.

3. Provide groups with adequate time to discuss critical-thinking questions. Groups generally need three to seven minutes to discuss each critical-thinking question. Circulate throughout the room to monitor group discussion.

Less Is More

Set a time limit for small-group discussion to encourage purposeful, focused discussion.

History Alive!

Facilitating Dynamic Whole-Class Discussion

After groups have had adequate time to discuss and write answers to a critical-thinking question, students are ready for class discussion. By this time, the small groups have generated a wealth of ideas for presenters to share with the class. The challenge is to facilitate the discussion so that the different points of view are brought forth in a lively, engaging fashion. This encourages students to consider new, more sophisticated ideas.

To begin class discussion, ask presenters from three groups to share their answers. Usually the ideas of the three presenters will vary; this is desirable. To hear all points of view and to create intellectual controversy, elicit responses from the other presenters. Rather than simply asking them to recite their answers, use any of these ways to inspire rich discussion:

- Ask if there are any presenters whose ideas are dramatically different than those already stated.
- Allow two presenters with diametrically opposed responses to argue their points.
- Ask a presenter who has not yet spoken to consider the ideas already mentioned and explain which point he or she most agrees with and most disagrees with.
- If the discussion is one-sided and only brings forth one point of view, promote deeper discussion by acting incredulous and arguing the unheard perspective.

As the class discussion unfolds, expect long response times—from thirty seconds to a minute or more—from presenters. The unfortunate by-product of this is that some presenters may not have the opportunity to share their answers fully or at all. If a group's presenter did not get a chance to speak, make sure you call on that group's presenter on the next critical-thinking question.

Three Outstanding Response Groups Activities

Use these three Response Groups activities to spur your creativity in designing lessons that spark energetic, rich discussion involving all students.

☐ How Far Have We Come Since Seneca Falls?

This Response Groups activity, introduced at the beginning of the chapter, highlights gender issues—a topic students love to talk about. Students read passages from the Declaration of Sentiments, a document written by women reformers at the Seneca Falls convention. Using data on American women today and their own experience, groups discuss the extent to which these grievances have been redressed today. They use a spectrum labeled *Grievance Totally Redressed* and *Grievance Not Redressed* to help quantify their answers. Lively debate focuses on whether equality exists for women today in politics, employment, status, education, and moral standards.

Encourage Active Listening

As presenters from each Response Group share their group's findings with the class, require them to start with a comment such as: "I agree/disagree with your group's ideas because. . . ." This will encourage students to listen carefully to each other and to direct their comments to each other instead of to you.

"Before and after Response Groups activities that create emotional class discussion, I remind my students not to allow intellectual disagreements to become personal or divisive. This allows for heated controversy, but does not undermine the feeling of cooperation and trust I try to establish in each class."

Vern Cleary,
High School Teacher

Chapter 5

A group engages in lively debate, focusing on whether equality exists for women today in politics, employment, status, education, and moral standards.

Favorite Features

- Students make connections between past and present.
- Use of manipulatives on spectrums increases student involvement.
- The activity uses rich primary sources.
- Substantive women's issues—historical and current—are discussed.
- Students are highly motivated to debate gender issues.

☐ The Cuban Missile Crisis: You Make the Call

This activity, mentioned earlier in this chapter, can be used in either a U.S. or world history class to teach the dramatic stages of the Cuban missile crisis. Groups assume the role of presidential advisors, examine photographs from military archives, and discuss four issues: (1) Why are the missile sites a concern? (2) Prioritize which course of action—ignore the sites, demand that the Soviets disassemble them, enact a naval blockade, bomb the sites, declare war on Cuba—the Kennedy administration should take. (3) Was Kennedy's actual response the most appropriate action? (4) Analyze the political cartoon (following the resolution of the missile crisis) and discuss the implications of such tense international encounters in the nuclear age.

"I never realized how tough it was to be the president of the United States! The president has to listen and decide among so many different points of view."
High School Student

Favorite Features

- Compelling historical photos are featured.
- Spirited discussions arise from the variety of perspectives on the interpretation of historical images.
- Students use problem-solving skills to attempt to resolve a complex historical crisis.

History Alive!

The ambiguity of political cartoons such as this one makes for intense Response Group discussions.

- After attempting to resolve it themselves, students are highly motivated to learn about the missile crisis.
- Global implications of the arms race are discussed.

☐ Comparing the Plights of the Homeless and of Medieval Serfs

This Response Groups activity, which was briefly referred to earlier, enables students to compare aspects of the lives of European serfs with those of contemporary homeless Americans. Groups see comparative slides depicting the food, shelter, clothing, and personal security of both serfs and the homeless. In addition, they receive primary and secondary source material about these aspects of the lives of serfs and the homeless. Students use this information to evaluate the plight of each and determine which had a better living situation. This leads to discussion on how feudal society protected individual rights and took responsibility for all members of the community. Students also discuss the role of the U.S. government in helping the homeless.

Chapter 5

Contrasting historic and contemporary images, like these of Medieval serfs and homeless Americans, can lead to rich discussions.

Favorite Features

- Students make connections between the past and present.
- Images and written resources give students a wealth of knowledge on which to base discussion.
- The issues raised are highly provocative.
- Students begin to compare the relative merits of feudalism and capitalism and their ability to provide individual security.
- Students are motivated to learn more about government policy regarding homelessness.

CHAPTER 6

Strategy Six: Writing for Understanding

To write forcefully and in detail about history, students need interactive experiences about which to write. Writing for Understanding activities tap into students' multiple abilities so that all learners—even those with lesser linguistic skills—have something memorable to write about. Creating purposeful writing assignments—such as writing an oral history on the legacy of the civil-rights movement, haiku on the internment of Japanese-Americans during World War II, a eulogy for the Mayan civilization, or a letter to the editor of a colonial newspaper commenting on the Boston Massacre—motivates students to write with style and meaning.

Eleventh grader Julia Adler enjoys writing. But in her traditional history classes, she found that writing assignments were vague and predictable. "Typically, we were told to write all we knew about some king we had studied," she explains. "The problem with assignments like that is I didn't know what to write about." When Julia was assigned research papers with few guidelines and expected to repeat facts she found in the library, she often would add imaginary dialogue to make the task more interesting. "You don't learn much just by rewriting plain facts that you have read or heard about," she says.

Julia's experience changed when she entered a class that used the Writing for Understanding approach. During a unit on the civil-rights movement, she was required to write a dialogue between Martin Luther King and Malcolm X. The goal was for students to portray their understanding of the differences in the philosophies of the two civil-rights leaders. Prior to writing the dialogue, they had a variety of multiple-ability experiences that gave them information about the civil-rights movement and the ideas of the two men. Students imagined the pain of discrimination in an Experiential Exercise, participated in an Interactive Slide Lecture on the major achievement of the movement, and read and discussed primary source materials on King and Malcolm X. Immediately before writing the

History Alive!

dialogue, students engaged in a pre-writing activity designed to give them ideas for the dialogue. Working in pairs, students assumed the roles of King and Malcolm X and responded in character to prompts from the teacher, such as "Integration into a racist system won't work" or "Separation is no different than segregation." Initially, Julia and her classmates were skeptical about the role-play.

By the time she sat down to her assignment, Julia was well prepared. "I really understood the ideas of Martin Luther King and Malcolm X through the different activities. That's why I put more effort into the dialogue than I would have put into a regular essay assignment." From Julia's dialogue:

> The room was bathed in the light of the fire. It was a sort of office, with an oaken desk with high-backed chairs and mahogany bookshelves lining two walls.... Through the door strode two men, chatting amiably.
>
> *Malcolm X:* Martin, I've been meaning to talk to you about this for awhile. I think that you're going about the civil rights movement the wrong way.... This policy of nonviolence just seems a bit irrational. It's kind of like saying, "Go ahead and whip me, beat me down, just like you've done for centuries. I don't mind."
>
> *King:* Our nonviolence policies have helped us accomplish so much. Sit-ins, marches, demonstrations, and those freedom rides . . . they show that we are unified, that we will not lie still while they oppress us. It also shows how strongly we believe in this cause, what we know is right, and we shall endure any amount of pain for this cause; that we shall not stoop to violence, because that would be on the level of those who are against us, and that would destroy our cause politically and socially.
>
> *Malcolm X:* We all know this but the time is NOW. We have been using nonviolent tactics for years and, yes, it has brought results, but the results come so slowly.
>
> *King:* Malcolm, I know that things may not have been happening very quickly in the past few years, but look at it from the time scale of one hundred years, two hundred years. For two centuries the black man had been denied his rights as a citizen, first with slavery, then with oppression and segregation. Segregation is what most white people grew up with and were taught to believe.... You must understand how deep this vein of racism runs in America, and what a hard task desegregation is.
>
> *Malcolm X:* That's another thing I really don't agree with you about. Why desegregate? What if we fight for, and get, our own power, and our own businesses, and restaurants, that are the same as the white's. Why do we have to go to the whites and beg to be let into their establishments. Even if we finally get into them, and are allowed to be in the same room with them, they will still treat us badly, giving us lower quality food in restaurants, and worse tables, and lower-paying jobs or all sorts of devious little things that cannot be pinned down to complain about.
>
> *King:* Malcolm, one of the ideas behind desegregation is so that the whites will be able to, or will be forced to, associate with us and see that we are people.... If they know us and have been around us for awhile, they can realize for themselves that racism is wrong, because we are their equals, just painted differently by the hand of God.

"I put more effort into the dialogue than I would have put into a regular essay assignment."
Julia Adler

Chapter 6

You can project slides of images to add realism as students role play different historical figures discussing key issues.

Julia attributes her successful dialogue—which demonstrated a clear understanding of the salient differences between King and Malcolm X—to the style of the assignment, which allowed her to make the dialogue realistic. She was also able to draw on the rich experiences that preceded the assignment to lend historical detail to her writing.

Writing as a Key to Learning in Social Studies

In the conventional history classroom, writing is used almost exclusively for assessment. While it is valuable to have students demonstrate what they learn through essays, test questions, or position papers, writing assignments should also be used to facilitate learning. Consider writing not as an end itself, but as access to learning. Writing can help your students learn history in these ways:

■ **Writing challenges students to clarify, organize, and express what they have learned.** When students are asked to verbalize their understanding of a historical issue, they often respond with vague, unorganized ideas. Requiring students to put their thoughts in writing challenges them to have explicit, detailed, and tangible ideas. After a study of the aftermath of the Civil War and Reconstruction, for example, students might have a general opinion about the present-day condition of African Americans. But when required to write a letter to Frederick Douglass about the issue—citing historical and

"Through lots of different types of writing assignments I realized that history is something that we need to understand by asking 'why' and 'how.' History can be an enjoyable learning experience."
High School Student

"Perhaps the most basic thing that can be said about human memory, after a century of research, is that unless detail is placed in a structured pattern, it is easily forgotten."[1]
Jerome Bruner

"One of the most common errors of beginning writers is the failure to root their generalizations in the world of experience. If the writer cannot readily cite specific examples, he had better question the truth of the general statement."[2]
Richard E. Young, Alton L. Becker, and Kenneth L. Pike

contemporary evidence—students are forced to clarify their ideas, to organize what they have learned, and to express their ideas coherently.

- **Writing requires students to analyze and synthesize.** Writing can be used to allow students to analyze historical events or to synthesize a large body of information. High-level thinking enables students to draw conclusions, to make connections between the past and present, and to develop informed opinions. At the conclusion of a unit on the Great Depression, for example, you might have students study poverty in the United States today. They could analyze pictures of individuals living in poverty, examine data on current economic trends, and synthesize their knowledge of the Depression, the New Deal, and contemporary poverty by writing a coherent plan suggesting a course of action to alleviate poverty in America.

- **Writing enables students to reach deeper understanding as they draw on previous learning for supporting detail.** Too often students make generalizations or express opinions about historical events without supporting detail or fact. Having students write about history is an excellent way to teach them the necessity of supporting their arguments with solid historical evidence and of carefully reviewing past events for deeper meaning. Assigning a position paper on whether European colonization benefited or hurt Africa, for example, forces students to analyze what they learned, to formulate an argument, and to support it with historical detail.

- **Ownership of written products motivates students to excel.** Students invest more time and energy in learning history if they are challenged to write creatively. If you encourage your students to develop their individual voices, their writing will become a form of self-expression rather than just a chronicle of facts. Students might learn about the plight of Chinese immigrants who were detained on Angel Island by viewing slides, listening to primary source accounts about life in the detention center, and reading the poetry Chinese immigrants wrote on the walls of the processing center. Students could then write and illustrate their own poems describing the experiences and feelings of detainees on Angel Island.

- **The writing process makes students refine their ideas.** The writing process—brainstorming, writing rough drafts, revising, and editing—requires focused thinking and precise expression. Whereas the spoken word is transitory, a written idea can be reviewed, revised, and embellished. The process of writing a polished, well-supported piece leads to greater understanding of a topic. Students might think carefully about the Lewis and Clark journey, for example, by assuming the role of William Clark and writing a journal entry about his expedition. Prompted by illustrations from the journey and a word bank of key terms from Clark's journal, students could write a first draft, share and critique their drafts in small groups, and then read the best pieces aloud and compare them to Clark's actual writings.

Chapter 6

An American having struck a Bear but not killed him, escapes into a Tree.

Students write about the Lewis and Clark journey by assuming the role of William Clark and writing a journal about his expedition as you prompt them with illustrations, like this one from Clark's own journal.

Basing Writing on Multiple-Ability Experiences

Writing in the conventional classroom generally reveals that most students do not have much to say about the history they are taught. Essays, opinion pieces, and test answers often lack historical detail, original style, and creative expression. At best, most writing efforts tend to be a simple summation of memorized facts.

To facilitate powerful writing in history, students need a variety of memorable, interactive experiences on which to base their writing. These activities must tap into multiple abilities so that all learners—even those with lesser linguistic skills—have something to say. As students participate in these activities, they learn history, develop ideas, and form opinions before they begin formal writing. Donald Murray[3] argues that a critical "pressure that moves [writers] forward toward the first draft is increasing information about the subject." When students see powerful slides, role-play, discuss a controversial issue, or act out a moment in history, they are beginning the writing process. The sadness in a slave spiritual or the visible destruction of Hiroshima evokes emotions, thoughts, and questions—the essence of what drives people to put words on paper.

Following is an example of how you could sequence lessons on the Great Depression to prepare students to write an autobiographical sketch of an individual from that time. Notice how the activities tap into a wide variety of abilities.

First, students view (visual-spatial), discuss (linguistic, interpersonal), and act out (body-kinesthetic, intrapersonal) a series of slides during an Interactive Slide Lecture that chronicles the coming of the Depression. Throughout the activity they record notes (linguistic). In an Experiential Exercise detailed in

"If a child can be encouraged to make a discovery nonverbally and then verbalize his feelings, he will actually be practicing the creative process."
Thomas Blakeslee

History Alive!

Chapter 3, after the teacher pretends to lose some of the class's quizzes, students experience some of the pain victims of bank failures felt (intrapersonal). Then students work in pairs (interpersonal) on a Social Studies Skill Builder to graph (logical-mathematical) key economic factors—unemployment, gross national product, stock prices, farm prices, bank failures—of the economic collapse. Finally, during a Problem-Solving Groupwork activity, students work in groups (interpersonal) to create a minidrama (body-kinesthetic, intrapersonal) about how individuals were impacted by the Depression. They base the minidramas on images of the time (visual-spatial) and primary and literary source material (linguistic). As the minidramas are presented, students take notes (linguistic) on the various ways people were affected by the Depression.

In this sequence of activities, students learned through images, dramatizations, words, graphs, and simulations, and now have a plethora of information, ideas, feelings, and impressions—plus their own writing from their notes—on which to base on an autobiographical sketch of a fictitious figure from the Depression. The experiences give students empathy for Depression victims and specific details to include in their writing. Eleventh grader Colleen Abastillas was able to convey the pain and shame of a grocery store owner whose business had failed: "People just didn't have the money to buy things, not even food. . . . Instead of having workers sell my apples, I was the one out on the corner selling what I had left. This was the only way I could support my family. I felt so ashamed, I could do nothing but bow my head down. . . . The one thing I could not tolerate was charity. Bread trucks came giving out free food, and I couldn't stand the thought of depending on anyone else, but me."

Give your students a variety of information, ideas, feelings, and impressions through multiple-ability experiences to create autobiographic sketches—rich with historical detail—of people impacted by the Depression.

Get It While It's Fresh

Ask students to begin writing during or immediately after an Experiential Exercise or other multiple-ability task. When students write while in the midst of a classroom experience, their writing takes on the emotions of the moment.

"The student writer's most important inner resources are words to use in talking about personal experience. Start with what they know and feel—and in their own words."[4]

Dan Kirby and Tom Liner

Chapter 6

Creating Writing Assignments with Purpose

Purposeful writing assignments—dialogues, poetry, stories, newspaper eulogies, speeches, letters—motivate students to write with style and meaning. While traditional essays and position papers are appropriate for some topics, giving students a wider variety of writing activities promotes experimentation and makes writing more exciting and novel. Here are twelve different forms of writing that will challenge your students to write creatively and in detail about history.

- **Encourage students to write a dialogue between two historical figures that highlights opposing viewpoints.** Ask students to write dialogues in a conversational tone and to include the salient points for each speaker. For example, students might write a dialogue between a turn-of-the-century worker and his boss that not only focuses on typical worker's grievances—long work hours, low pay, unsafe working conditions—but also on management's concerns: competition, low productivity, worker absenteeism. Other suitable subjects are Soviet and American ideology during the Cold War, a Loyalist and a Patriot in 1776, Mansa Musa and Sunni Ali Ber, a Japanese courtier and a samurai warrior, Thomas Hobbes and John Locke, and Harriet Tubman and John C. Calhoun.

- **Teach students to write essays that includes a clear thesis statement, topic sentences for each paragraph, supporting detail, and a strong conclusion.** Essay assignments are best used when you want students to analyze or synthesize a large body of history. For example, you might want students to write an essay highlighting the conflicts that led to the split between the Orthodox Church and the Roman Catholic Church. Other ideas for essay assignments include a comparison of European and Japanese feudalism, an analysis of whether the Civil War was inevitable, an exploration of the historical roots of tension in the Middle East, and a comparison of Native-American and colonial land adaptations.

- **Captivate interest in the past by having students write eulogies extolling the virtues of a prominent historical figure or civilization.** Eulogies should include formal language, a brief summary about the person (or civilization), an elaboration of that person's legacy, and a conclusion about how the achievements of that person still impact the world today. A eulogy to the Roman Empire, for example, would include a summary of the accomplishments of the Roman Empire and a list of how those accomplishments—in areas such as law, architecture, art, government, and sports—are seen in the world today. Other people and civilizations students can write eulogies about include Kublai Khan, Hiawatha, Abraham Lincoln, Susan B. Anthony, Socrates, the Soviet Union, the Roman Empire, and the Mayan civilization.

- **Focus interest on controversial historical figures by having students create a Hero/Wanted poster that both praises and criticizes a figure from the past.** Each poster should have an illustration, background information, and a list of the person's accomplishments and "crimes." Students will use critical-thinking skills to explore dual perspectives. For example, a poster on Nelson Mandela might list his accomplishments—awakening the

---

Prompting Inspired Writing

When a writing assignment is compelling enough for students to care about, inspired writing follows.

"Writing a eulogy about Joaquin Murietta made me think about how Mexicans must have felt after the war with Mexico. I could really feel history because I had to put myself in Murietta's place."
Middle School Student

History Alive!

conscience of South Africa, building a powerful political movement, focusing world attention on the social problems of his nation—and his alleged crimes: inciting South Africans to riot, arming members of the African National Congress, making South Africa look disharmonious to the rest of the world. Other poster candidates include Chingis Khan, Martin Luther, Christopher Columbus, Joseph Stalin, Mao Tse Tung, Huey Long, Al Capone, and Indira Gandhi.

■ **Show students how to write historical journal entries that bring to life the events of the past.** Encourage students to adopt a narrative format that uses the colloquial language of the era. Each entry should include the correct historical date and a detailed account of the historical figure's feelings and experiences. Use visual or musical prompts to give students ideas. For example, to encourage students to write journal entries about the Lewis and Clark expedition, show them a series of illustrations from William Clark's own journal and a map detailing the journey's route. For each illustration, ask students to write an entry from Clark's perspective and in the present tense—as if they were there. Other ideas for journal writing include a report from a British journalist on social life in the American colonies, a journal from a participant in the French Revolution, a travel log from the Silk Road, and excerpts from the diary of a civil-rights activist who participated in the Freedom March.

■ **Challenge students to write letters that convey the feelings of a historical figure to a particular audience.** Letters are written from the point of view of someone who witnessed history and then related those events to a specific audience. Encourage students to use descriptive narrative and to integrate as much accurate historical information as possible. Motivate them with pre-writing activities that make them feel as though they have witnessed history. During a unit on World War I, for example, place students on the floor between rows of desks representing trenches, and show them a series of slides depicting the horrors of warfare on Europe's western front. As they are sitting in the trenches, have them write two letters home, one to their family and one to a trusted friend. Later they can discuss how the tone of each letter depended on the audience for which it was written. Other historical personas they might adopt include an Arab traveler writing home about a visit to Timbuktu, Dorothea Lange writing to President Roosevelt chronicling the plight of victims of the Depression, or the bomber pilot writing home about dropping an atom bomb on Hiroshima.

■ **Have students write a memorandum to a historical leader that recommends a course of action or a new policy.** Memoranda should be properly formatted with To, From, Re, Date; an executive summary of the action or policy recommendation; and a list of supporting reasons. For example, students might assume the role of Sor Juana Inés de la Cruz, a great writer and Spanish nun living in Mexico in the sixteenth century, sending a memo to the King of Spain deploring the unequal position of women in Mexican society. Among the evidence she might cite is that women received little if any schooling, that nuns were expected to play a less public role than priests, and that women writers could find no publishers for their work. Other possibilities include memos to the president regarding poverty in

---

Share *Your* Writing

Write with your students to show them you value the skill. Create models of the assignment ahead of time, or do the assignment with them and display your work with theirs.

"Good journal writing is fishing in the river of your mind."[5]
Dan Kirby and Tom Liner

"My students' letters home from the trenches were so rich with emotion and detail that I was almost brought to tears as I read them."
Beth Bernstein, High School Teacher

Chapter 6

America today, to Portugal's Prince Henry the Navigator about whether or not to trade with Africa, to a British viceroy regarding India's demand for independence, and to President Truman regarding whether or not to use the atomic bomb on Japan.

■ **Help students understand bias by assigning them to write a newspaper editorial about a historical event.** Editorials should clearly state their position on the issue, use language that reflects the bias of the newspaper, and contain supporting evidence. For example, students might assume the role of an Islamic editorial writer commenting on the Crusades. Far from a Holy War, students would write about the Crusades as a military invasion of Islamic territory and as a calculated war of genocide against the Muslim people. Other opinion pieces might include an editorial from a South Carolina newspaper on the eve of the Civil War, an editorial on the Boston Tea Party from a colonial newspaper, and an editorial from a Catholic newspaper on the Reformation.

■ **Teach students to interview individuals who experienced recent history and to write oral histories afterward.** Prepare students by conducting a mock interview in class, asking well-conceived, thoughtful questions. Then have students make a list of twenty to thirty questions to ask their interviewee. Carefully discuss ways—such as being polite, making eye contact, asking several questions, practicing active-listening skills—students can make the interviewee feel more comfortable. After they have conducted their interview, their write-up should include an introduction of the interviewee, direct quotes and paraphrasing from the interview, and an analysis of the interviewee's perspective on the historical event. One powerful oral history students can research, interview, and write about is the Vietnam War. Require students to find someone who was affected by the war—a protester, a conscientious objector, a soldier, a parent who lost a son or daughter, a local politician who opposed the war—and then ask such questions as: What do you remember about the war? How did it affect you personally? Did you support or oppose the war? What do you remember most about the war? How did the war change our nation? Other topics for oral histories include the Depression, World War II, the civil-rights movement, the Cold War, recent immigration, and the social rebellion of the late 1960s.

"Oral histories have been a tremendous success with my students. Initially, students are reluctant and a little scared to take the risk to interview someone. But after they talk to someone and record original historical findings, they produce fabulous writing and have a real sense of accomplishment."
Mike Warner,
High School Teacher

■ **Encourage students to write with empathy about an event or group in history through poetry and song lyrics.** Students should adhere to a specific style of poetry or song lyric and use descriptive language that evokes emotion and makes direct references to the topic. For example, after showing slides about the internment of Japanese-Americans during World War II, challenge students to write haiku from the perspective of those interned, using evocative language and emotion. Other possibilities include illuminated poems on medieval Europe, a spell-out poem about Montezuma, lyrics to a *corrido,* or folk song, about the Mexicano heritage in the Southwest, and adapted lyrics to "My Country 'Tis of Thee" from the perspective of a turn-of-the-century populist.

"The haiku my students produced about Japanese-American internment were amazing. The students illustrated their poems, and I posted them on the wall for all to see. They left a lasting impression."
Deborah Whitson,
High School Teacher

■ **Teach students how to write position papers that take a definitive stand on controversial issues.** Position papers should include an introduction framing a controversial issue, a clear statement of the student's

History Alive!

Students as Published Authors

Publishing student writing enlarges the audience, motivates students, and creates the need for real communication. You might post student writing in class, photocopy it for others to read, or encourage students to give dramatic readings of their written work. You might join with other teachers to print and bind oral histories for the entire school, submit pieces to the school paper, or display writing in the halls. Or you might help students submit writing to the local paper or writing contests.

position, supporting evidence, compelling arguments against the opposing viewpoint, and a persuasive conclusion. For example, students might write that the grievances aired in the late nineteenth century by women reformers at Seneca Falls have not been redressed today. As evidence, they might include the fact that today women earn approximately sixty-seven cents for every dollar a man earns, that women do seventy-eight percent of the housework in the United States, and that only ten percent of management positions are held by women. Other position papers might be on whether the United States should be praised or condemned for its actions in the Cold War, whether Hernan Cortés and his men were guilty of genocide, whether Africa benefited from European colonialism, or whether Russians were better off under communism.

■ **Show students how to integrate newfound historical knowledge into a creative story.** Stories should have a clear plot, a descriptive setting, characters, a conflict, and a resolution. Challenge students to integrate historical information into their stories. For example, after students have listened to Hopi music from rain-dance ceremonies, ask them to write a story about how the rain god affected life in the Southwest. Their story should include aspects of the geography, history, and social life of the Southwest; and the elements of a good story, such as character, conflict, and resolution. Other possible topics include a tale based on African folk tales, a story about life without the Bill of Rights, a story in the style of the Canterbury tales, and a story about life as a serf on a medieval manor.

Show this slide of the Pueblo Walpi where Hopi lived in Arizona and play music to inspire your students to write a creative story about Native Americans.

Chapter 6

Writing as a Process

Use the experience and innovation of English teachers as you incorporate writing into your classes. Frustrated with traditional instructional methods like sentence diagramming and grammar drills, many English teachers looked to the writing of professionals. They found successful writers use a process based on writing from experience, revising original drafts, and careful editing, and know that writing takes time, patience, and revision. Likewise, students in history classes need to honor the writing process. To demonstrate their understanding of a topic effectively, students must be allowed to generate ideas through pre-writing activities, to create original drafts, and to revise and edit them. This investment in time yields powerful writing and increased learning. Here is an effective, six-step writing process you can teach your students.

1. Engage students in pre-writing activities. To write forcefully about history, students need concrete ideas and a way to organize them. Pre-writing activities help students generate specific ideas. For example, you might put them thorough a role-play that simulates discrimination and immediately afterwards have them write down all their ideas and feelings. Students might also access concrete ideas by reviewing their notes from previous assignments; role-playing dialogues between historical figures; participating in panel discussions to explore different viewpoints on controversial events; examining historical photos, illustrations, or art; listening to music that represents an idea from the past; or working with a partner or small group to brainstorm ideas. Once students have generated ideas, they must organize and plan their writing. Model several methods for organizing ideas. You might have them put their ideas into outline form by topic and subtopic, or into a spoke diagram with the main idea in the center surrounded by supporting details.

2. Give clear expectations and precise guidelines for writing assignments. Confusion is a major obstacle to coherent writing. Give your students a handout that clearly states guidelines and deadlines for all parts of the assignment.

3. Have students write a first draft. Once students finish organizing their ideas, have them write down all of their ideas and experiment with organizational structure. Stress that while this draft does not have to be polished, it must be complete. Collect the drafts and give students credit for their work. Read them quickly, and note your suggestions.

4. Use peer feedback groups. Divide students into heterogeneous groups of three or four. Before students move into groups, emphasize that feedback should be honest, constructive, and specific. Once students are in groups, encourage them to read their papers aloud to the group. While one student reads, the others should ask for clarification. As comments are made, writers should note the suggestions directly on their drafts. After listening to a paper, student respondents should fill in the Peer Feedback Checklists (see p. 118) and give them to the writer.

"There is something antic about creating, although the enterprise be serious. And there is a matching antic spirit that goes with writing about it, for if ever there was a silent process, it is the creative one. Antic and serious and silent."[6]
Jerome Bruner

"Writing has got to be an act of discovery . . . I write to find out what I am thinking about."
Edward Albee

A New Beginning

During peer revision time, ask students to move the concluding paragraph of their first draft to the beginning to act as an introductory paragraph. Have them read this new introduction to their peer group for feedback. Sometimes writers finally get to what they really want to say only at the conclusion.

Peer Feedback Checklist

Respondent's Name ——————————— Writer's Name ———————————
Assignment ——————————————— Date ————— Class/Per. —————

Scoring scale: 1 2 3 4 5
                 Poor Average Excellent

FIRST DRAFT　　　　　**Score (1 – 5)**　　　　**Comments and Suggestions**

Did the writer:

1. Write clear sentences?

2. Cite accurate historical information?

3. Use supporting details and examples?

4. Use a proper format and organization?

5. Create a logical, coherent piece of writing?

Additional feedback

6. Pick out three sentences you particularly like. What do you like most about them?

7. What is your favorite part of this piece? Why?

8. What should the writer do to improve the piece?

© Addison-Wesley Publishing Company, Inc.

Chapter 6

Students work in peer feedback groups to edit each others' writing.

5. Require students to make revisions. Students should use the feedback they received from you and from their peers to revise their original draft.

6. Have students edit their final draft. Before turning in their final drafts, require students to have their papers edited. The writer can fill out the "Editing Checklist" on page 120, or you can have the writer get someone else—a classmate, a parent, or another teacher—to complete it. Tell students that if their editor finds many errors, they must rewrite the paper. Minor changes can be made directly on the final draft. Students should attach the completed "Editing Checklist" to their final draft.

Hints for Managing the Paper Load

Assessing Writing for Understanding activities can be taxing and time-consuming, especially if you expect to thoroughly grade every piece of writing. Here are alternatives that will give your students substantive feedback while saving you from a crushing paper load.

1. Use Peer Feedback Groups during the writing process to minimize the time it takes to grade rough drafts.
2. Have students write in a first draft/final draft format. Grade only the final draft.
3. Use focused grading. Grade for only one or two specific parts of the assignment other than historical accuracy, such as organization or persuasiveness. At the beginning of each assignment, clearly define the criteria for assessment.
4. Use a portfolio system in which students keep selected samples of their work throughout the semester. After students complete several Writing for Understanding assignments, have them choose two or three to further revise. Thoroughly grade these writings.

Ready-Made Portfolios

At the end of the writing project, collect all drafts, notes, and checklists—stapled together, with the final draft on top. Students (and you) will see how much work they have done to get to the final draft. These writing assignments can go into students' portfolios.

History Alive!

5. Stagger due dates for major writing assignments among your classes, and don't set them immediately before the end of a grading period.
6. Create a Writing Evaluation Form (see page 121) to allow student to assess themselves. Tailor the form to the featured aspects of a particular assignment.

Editing Checklist

1. Describe the appearance of the paper. Is it typed? Well-formatted? Clean?

2. List any spelling errors.

3. List punctuation or capitalization suggestions.

4. Give examples of sentences that are hard to read, and offer alternatives.

5. Give examples of arguments that were not supported with details or examples, and suggest alternatives.

6. Comment on the paper's organization.

Editor's signature _____

© Addison-Wesley Publishing Company, Inc.

Writing Evaluation Form

Name _____

Assignment _____ Date _____

	Student Assessment	Teacher Assessment	Points
1. First draft completed on time.			
2. Helpful suggestions given in Peer Response Group to other writers.			
3. Revision notes made on first draft.			
4. Revisions incorporated into final draft.			
5. Careful editing of final draft for spelling, grammar, and punctuation errors.			
6. Final draft completed on time.			
7. Historical information used correctly.			
8. Ideas supported with detail.			
9. Sentences clear and understandable.			
10. Appropriate format and organization.			

Total

Student comments

Teacher comments

History Alive!

Three Outstanding Writing for Understanding Activities

Successful Writing for Understanding activities are content-appropriate, purposeful, based on multiple-ability experiences, and tailored to match the subject matter and your purpose. They require that you think of writing as more than an assessment of student knowledge, but as an opportunity to further student understanding of the content. Here are brief descriptions of three outstanding Writing for Understanding activities.

☐ Labor and Management Talk It Out

After learning about the Industrial Revolution and the working conditions in factories, students sit in pairs facing each other and assume the role of either a worker or a factory owner. The teacher prompts the "workers" by asking them to repeat in unison: "Why is pay so low in this factory?" "Workers" then engage in a debate with their partners. After a minute, the teacher stops the class and reads a line for the "factory owners," and the pairs once more debate. The teacher reads three or four lines for each character and then asks the students to switch roles. After the debate, students have plenty of ideas with which to write a turn-of-the-century dialogue between labor and management.

Favorite Features

- Students must take on the role of a historical figure and passionately defend his or her position.
- Students must switch roles, forcing them to argue both sides of an issue.
- The pre-writing activity gives students plenty of ideas to include in their dialogues.
- Students begin writing immediately after the activity. Their excitement and enthusiasm often translate into passionate writing.

Students assume the roles of labor and management to argue about working conditions in a turn-of-the-century factory. This pre-writing activity gives students a wealth of ideas to draw on.

Chapter 6

☐ Asian Immigration: The Chinese on Angel Island

This Writing for Understanding activity is part of a unit on turn-of-the-century immigration. Students write a three-stanza poem about the Chinese immigrant experience that focuses on the long wait many had at the detention center on Angel Island in San Francisco Bay. As a pre-writing activity, students stand in pairs next to a wall covered with pieces of butcher paper as they view slides and listen to the teacher detailing the history of Chinese immigrants in California. While looking at a slide of the Angel Island barracks and poems carved in the walls by the waiting immigrants, students hear primary source accounts of what being in the detention center was like and write several lines on the butcher paper, imagining the feelings of the immigrants. They then listen while the teacher reads several poems written by Chinese immigrants, and then compare their poems to the immigrants' poems. Students see several slides of life on Angel Island and write poetic lines for each scene, comparing their words to actual poems each time. After the slides, students walk past the poem-covered walls, reading the words of their classmates. The students are then ready to begin creating a more refined three-stanza poem.

Favorite Features

- Students empathize with Chinese immigrants when they hear the immigrants' poems and see detention-center conditions.
- Students have an opportunity to compare their poems to the immigrants' poems.
- Students are able to see and read the poems of their classmates.
- Before writing their final poem, students have many sources—photographs, stories from Chinese immigrants, the poems of Chinese immigrants and other students, and their own poetry—from which to glean ideas.

Students imagine the feelings of Chinese immigrants detained on Angel Island by viewing slides of the detention center, listening to a tape detailing the detainees' experiences, and writing poems on the walls, just as the detained immigrants did.

History Alive!

☐ A Letter Home from the Trenches

This Writing for Understanding activity could be used as part of a unit on World War I. After learning about the outbreak of World War I in an Interactive Slide Lecture, students feel the terrible sense of isolation and terror faced by soldiers as they crouch in "trenches" between rows of desks, view slides of the western front, hear excerpts from "All Quiet on the Western Front," and respond—verbally, physically, and in writing—to various situations soldiers faced in the trenches. Then, students receive facsimiles of "aerograms" and write a letter to their families describing their experiences on the warfront. Students are encouraged to use descriptive language to explain how they cope with the rigor of the lifestyle, to describe their living conditions, and to convey the physical and emotional trauma of trench warfare.

Favorite Features

- Students learn about the physical and emotional trauma of trench warfare through a variety of intelligences—body-kinesthetic, visual-spatial, linguistic, intrapersonal, and interpersonal.
- Students write immediately after they experience the trench war simulation so that their thoughts, feelings, and experiences are incorporated into their letters.
- Students write in cramped, uncomfortable conditions, which helps make the writing more realistic.
- Students recognize the need to tailor writing to the audience as they decide what details from the warfront would be appropriate to describe to their family.

Student write letters home from the trenches, describing the living conditions, the rigorous lifestyle, and the physical and emotional trauma of trench warfare.

PART 3

Tools for Implementing an Active Approach to Teaching History

CHAPTER 7

Creating a Tolerant, Cooperative Classroom

Teaching history in an interactive and engaging way necessitates creating a cooperative, tolerant classroom. In this environment students will learn to share ideas, to work together cooperatively, to tolerate differences, to disagree honestly, and to take risks—and all students will feel valued and respected. Such an environment is created by following a careful, step-by-step program of cooperative skill building. The lessons you teach your students about cooperation will serve them well not only in your class, but for the rest of their lives.

Most students and teachers are nervous, apprehensive, guarded, and sometimes scared when they enter a new class. But interactive, engaging, experiential, stimulating teaching cannot take place until students feel comfortable to share ideas, to take risks, to work cooperatively, to tolerate differences, and to disagree honestly with the teacher and their classmates. Purposeful steps must be taken to develop a sense of community in the classroom so that all learners feel valued, respected, and at ease. You must be willing to invest time—the equivalent of six to ten class periods spread over the course of the year—to develop a cooperative, tolerant environment. Your investment will yield powerful results:

- The class develops a sense of community and trust.
- All students feel valued and respected.
- Students interact more freely—and learn more—because they are safe from ridicule, putdowns, and condescension.
- Classroom management is proactive and consistent, rather than reactive and punitive.
- Students learn to tolerate differences, to respect ideas, and to appreciate diversity.
- You and your students develop a collaborative, rather than adversarial, relationship.
- You and your students feel comfortable about taking risks.

Small Investment, Big Reward

You must be willing to invest time to develop a cooperative, tolerant environment. This investment will yield greater learning throughout the rest of the year.

"My teacher takes time to greet his students each day, which makes them feel welcome."
Middle School Student

Greeting students as they enter your classroom makes them feel immediately welcome and sets the tone for a cooperative, tolerant classroom.

History Alive!

In a cooperative, tolerant classroom, students interact more freely and learn more because they feel safe to share ideas, to take risks, and to express themselves.

- Cooperative interaction is created and incorporated into whole-class instruction, groupwork activities, and paired work.
- Ethnic and cultural diversity is perceived as an opportunity, not a problem.

Ten steps for creating a cooperative, tolerant classroom follow. Use them as they appear, or adapt them to your own teaching style and the age and social skill levels of your students. However you use them, remember that creating a safe environment for learning is critical.

Step 1 Greet your students at the door every day as they enter your classroom.

Rationale Students like to be recognized for what they are—young people with a wide range of needs, interests, and feelings. Making time to say hello, smile, and converse with them demonstrates a respect for them as people, conveys a warmth students quickly recognize, and reinforces the notion of treating everyone with respect.

What to Do Explain to your students that you will greet them at the door so that you can make a personal connection with each of them every day. Stand by your classroom door between classes. As your students enter your classroom, greet them with a friendly Hello, Good morning, or How's it going? As the semester progresses and you know your students better, your banter with them will become more informed and less superficial. If you cannot be at the door on a given day, ask the first student who comes to class to greet the rest of the class for you.

When Start the first day of class, and do it every day.

Chapter 7

Step 2 **Explain to your students the three basic policies governing a cooperative, tolerant classroom.**

Rationale The key to creating a cooperative, tolerant classroom is to involve students in regulating their own behavior. The first step in granting students control over their own actions is to give them a set of simple but universal classroom rules. This will show them, for example, that you trust them to know that sharpening a pencil during a class discussion is not respectful behavior. You need not make a rule for every conceivable behavior—that would only send students the message that you don't trust them enough to know how to behave properly.

What to Do Tell students that classroom behavior will be governed by three policies, all based on your desire to have a tolerant, cooperative classroom. Explain that these are not punitive measures to control their behavior, but guidelines to help them build a sense of community. The three policies are:

1. Everyone, including the teacher, will be treated with respect.
2. Putdowns and purposely hurtful comments or actions will not be tolerated.
3. No one will be allowed to disrupt the learning process of anyone else.

Clarify what these policies mean to you. Give students specific examples of respectful behavior, intolerable putdowns, and disruptive actions. To describe respectful behavior you might explain how to disagree with someone in a positive way by using their name, restating their argument, and then giving your own position. To explain purposefully hurtful comments you might explicitly state that racist, sexist, and homophobic comments will not be tolerated. Explain why it is important to have a cooperative, tolerant environment. Frequently review these policies. Finally, and most importantly, model these behaviors throughout the course. If you do not set a convincing example, or if your behavior contradicts any of the three policies, your students will quickly ignore them.

When Introduce these policies the first day of class and review them every day of the first week, especially as new students come into class. Then review them every week or two during the year, especially as they connect to the cooperative skills training for groupwork (see step 6).

Step 3 **Allow students to engage in an ice-breaking activity to make them more comfortable with their new classmates.**

Rationale Students are often nervous and anxious as they try to adapt to a new setting and a new group of classmates. Until they feel relatively at ease, most students will not interact easily or be willing to take risks with each other. Many students, in fact, will not participate in class discussions until they are confident that their comments won't be belittled or quickly categorized as "wrong." As a result, it is crucial to invest a class period breaking social tension and beginning to build class rapport. The sooner students feel comfortable, the sooner meaningful learning can take place.

"The secret of education is respecting the pupil."
Ralph Waldo Emerson

"The best thing about this class was the openness. You could express yourself without fear of reprisal."
High School Student

History Alive!

Students circulate around the classroom introducing themselves and obtaining signatures from each other.

What to Do Give each student a copy of "Get the Autograph of Someone Who . . ." (see p. 131). Explain that students will need to obtain signatures from classmates who fit each of the thirty-five characteristics and that they can collect only two signatures per classmate. Thus, students must talk to at least eighteen different people. Tell them that before asking for a signature, they must introduce themselves (Hello, my name is . . .) and ask the person a question about the characteristic (Where outside of the state did you go this summer?). This allows students to learn the names of their classmates and prevents them from simply shoving the paper at somebody without any real interaction. Tell students that you, too, are available for signatures. You may even want to complete this activity with them.

After most students have thirty-five signatures, go through the categories to find out which students in the class fit each of the characteristics. This allows everyone to acknowledge the talents, interests, and experiences represented in the class. By the end of the period, you and the students will feel far more comfortable with one another.

When The second day of class. You may want to use similar rapport-building activities periodically to build and maintain the sense of community in the class.

Get the Autograph of Someone Who . . .

Find someone in the class who fits each of these thirty-five categories. Before you get an autograph, you must shake hands, introduce yourself (Hello, my name is . . .), and ask one question about the issues the person is signing. For example, if they sign the first category about leaving the state this summer, you might ask them: Where did you go? You can only collect two signatures from each person.

Get the autograph of someone who . . .

1. Left the state over the summer _____
2. Has the same shoe size as you _____
3. Likes to watch football _____
4. Likes to draw _____
5. Brushes with the same toothpaste you use _____
6. Has seen a play _____
7. Has had braces _____
8. Is wearing jeans _____
9. Is in another class with you _____
10. Is new to this school _____
11. Is from a different ethnic group than you _____
12. Has traveled to another country _____
13. Has the same color eyes as you _____
14. Cut a class last year _____
15. Was born outside the United States _____
16. Likes to dance _____
17. Has a unique hair style _____
18. Is tall _____
19. You have never spoken to before _____
20. Loves history _____
21. Hates history _____
22. Has surfed _____
23. Likes the outdoors _____
24. Has more than five brothers and sisters _____
25. Is an only child _____
26. Likes to sing _____
27. Speaks another language _____
28. Watches more than five videos a week _____
29. Likes to sit in the sun _____
30. Recycles newspapers _____
31. Has ridden a bike more than 25 miles _____
32. Changes their own motor oil _____
33. Chews gum _____
34. Likes Rap music _____
35. Plays on a sports team _____

© Addison-Wesley Publishing Company, Inc.

History Alive!

> "The future of America, in a globalized economy without a cold war, will rest with people who can think and act with informed grace across ethnic, cultural, linguistic lines."[1]
>
> Robert Hughes

Step 4 **Convince students that learning how to work with other students effectively will benefit them throughout their life.**

Rationale Students often need to be convinced that what they are learning is worthwhile, so explaining the short- and long-term benefits of cooperation is crucial. Cooperative learning is not only a sound, research-supported pedagogical approach, but also a means to teach students valuable "people skills" that will serve them in their workplace and their community, especially given our increasingly diverse population.

What to Do Make "Survey of Employers" into an overhead transparency.[2] Ask students this question: Other than job competency, what do you think most employers look for in an employee? Allow students a few minutes for discussion, then project the survey. Explain that the top three characteristics—dependability, positive attitude, and the ability to get along well with others—are not directly addressed in most schools' curriculum. Explain that throughout your class, they will have the opportunity to develop those attributes as they work with others on a variety of activities. In this way, not only will they be learning history, but also effective ways to work with others.

This step usually takes only ten to fifteen minutes. Just make it clear to students that you will be teaching not only the course content, but cooperative skills that will serve them long after the class is over.

When Do this sometime during the second week of the class, before you hold any formal small-group activities. You may also want to send a copy of "Survey of Employers" home to families.

Survey of Employers

Employers were asked this question: Other than job competency, what qualities do you desire in your employees?

Quality	Percentage of employers who said this quality was valued
Dependability	94%
Positive attitude	88
Ability to get along well with others	74
Ability to read	65
Ability to do basic arithmetic	56
Ability to read complex materials	22
Ability to handle complex math	10

Chapter 7

Step 5 **Teach students how to move efficiently and properly into different-size groups.**

Rationale While it may appear silly to teach students—particularly high school students—how to move their desks into groups, a fifteen- to twenty-minute investment pays dividends in time saved throughout the semester. The success of groupwork activities depends on students arranging their desks properly. Without clearly stated expectations about how to move into groups quickly, students can waste valuable class time arranging the room, socializing, and stalling. Students must move into groups and be prepared to work within sixty seconds. A brief training will accomplish this.

What to Do Tell your students they will be working in different-size groups throughout the course and must know how to move into groups efficiently. Explain that each time they move into groups, they should bring everything—backpacks, notebooks, pens, jackets—with them. Tell them that before they move, you will have explained with whom and where they will form their group and what materials they will need.

Explain the importance of group configuration. When working in pairs, students should arrange their desks side by side, with the sides of their desks touching, or facing one another, with the front edges touching. The activity will dictate which of the two arrangements they will use. For most other group sizes, the rule of desk arrangement is simply this: The corners of the desks must touch. This allows each student to face all group members.

With these expectations clear, allow students to practice moving into groups. Be prepared for them to think this exercise is silly at best and condescending at worst. Understand their feelings, and try to make the exercise game-like. If you don't go through this exercise, you may end up teaching it later, when you find it takes students fifteen minutes to set up for groups.

Randomly assign students to pairs and indicate where each pair should meet. You might want to project a classroom map on the overhead. Explain that they are to sit side by side and will need a pen and paper. When the directions are clear, say Go. Watch that their movement meets your expectations; you may want to time them. If necessary, explain what went wrong and have them repeat the process. Repeat the entire exercise for other group sizes, such as three, four, or five. Acknowledge that it is more difficult to arrange desks in larger groups than it is to put them in pairs.

When During the second or third week of the class, before you do any formal groupwork.

Step 6 **Use role-playing activities to teach your students cooperative skills.**

Rationale For groups to function cooperatively, students must know what it means to be cooperative. Too often teachers put students into groups and simply say, Cooperate. But many students lack social skills or have little experience working as a team; they must be taught expectations for cooperative interaction. Otherwise, you will find yourself continually reacting to inappropriate behavior.

What to Do Make an overhead transparency of "Cooperative Skills" (see p. 135). Explain to students that you will demonstrate the do's and don'ts of groupwork so they will have a clear idea of what is appropriate.

Train, Don't Strain

In an interactive classroom employing a variety of learning strategies, changing the arrangement of desks occurs frequently. Train your students to move their desks to avoid wasting your time.

"It seemed silly at first to be teaching high school students how to move their desks into exact arrangements. But now my students can move into different-size groups quickly and begin working without disruption or delay."
Dan Picardi,
High School Teacher

"Children have more need of models than of critics."
Joseph Joubert

History Alive!

Have four volunteers bring their desks to the front. Join the group and ask them to help you dramatize three role plays, each a quick discussion of a fun topic. As you role play with them, model specific inappropriate behaviors. After each role play, discuss what went wrong in the group and reveal the corresponding appropriate behaviors from the transparency. Then model the appropriate behaviors.

Role Play 1: Preparing for Groupwork

Ask the volunteers to discuss this question with you: What would you do if someone gave you a million dollars? As you sit with the group, model inappropriate behaviors for a minute or two: Sit with your eyes looking downward. Don't say anything. Fumble through a bookbag. Move your desk and turn your body away from the others. Stop, and ask the class: What behaviors were inappropriate? How did the group feel about your behavior? What might have caused you to act the way you did? Has anyone ever acted this way when they were uncomfortable in a new group? After the discussion, reveal Cooperative Skills 1 through 5 one at a time, and carefully discuss each:

1. Break tension and be friendly. Point out that perhaps the easiest way to break tension is to be friendly—with a warm smile, a polite Hello or How are you, a compliment such as I like your shirt, an inoffensive joke, or a personal introduction.

2. Learn and use names. Make clear the importance of introductions and teach students to shake each others' hands and say: Hello, my name is. . . . Remind students that if they forget a name it is okay to ask again. Explain that using names personalizes interaction and is the first step in building relationships because it reduces anonymity and conveys warmth.

3. Arrange desks properly. Point out that a desk that is outside the group connotes disinterest and disengagement.

A teacher models inappropriate groupwork behavior to dramatize how uncooperative behavior can disrupt the groupwork process.

4. Use positive body language. Nonverbal communication is often more powerful than spoken communication, so students should be aware of what their body language is saying. Demonstrate how to sit upright in a chair and how to squarely face other group members. Tell students that slouching, holding their head in their hands, and angling their body away from the group suggests an attempt to disengage. Tell them to be aware, however, of cultural norms that may affect body language; they and you shouldn't be too quick to interpret what may appear to be negative body language.

5. Be aware of eye contact. Students should be conscious of how their eye contact can affect interaction, and they should do their best to maintain appropriate eye contact while communicating. They and you should be considerate, however, of cultural differences that sometimes affect an individual's norms about eye contact.

At the end of the discussion, role-play the appropriate behaviors with the volunteer group.

Role Play 2: Creating a Supportive Atmosphere

Ask the four volunteers to discuss this question with you: What will each of you be doing ten years from now? As you sit with the group, model inappropriate behaviors for a minute or two: Don't listen to other group members. Interrupt students as they speak. Make negative comments. Do little to encourage relevant discussion. Stop, and ask the class: What behaviors were inappropriate? How did group members feel about your behavior? Why did you behave they way you did? What happens to the supportive atmosphere in a group when someone behaves inappropriately? After the class discussion, reveal Cooperative Skills 6 and 7 one at a time, and carefully discuss each.

Cooperative Skills

1. Break tension and be friendly.
2. Learn and use names.
3. Arrange desks properly.
4. Use positive body language.
5. Be aware of eye contact.
6. Listen to others and take turns giving ideas.
7. Use positive comments, encourage, and express appreciation.
8. Be helpful and assist each other.
9. Disagree in an agreeable way.
10. Stay on task.

© Addison-Wesley Publishing Company, Inc.

History Alive!

6. Listen to others and take turns giving ideas. Make sure the facilitator, or whoever is in charge of eliciting ideas from other group members, allows everyone to voice ideas. Point out the importance of having everyone contribute. Tell students to ask clarifying questions, such as: Why do you believe that? or How does that affect you? so that they better understand one another.

7. Use positive comments, encourage, and express appreciation. Emphasize that the most effective teams and organizations use positive reinforcement and have a supportive atmosphere. Point out that the more team cohesion in a group, the better the work will be and the more fun students will have.

At the end of the discussion, role-play the appropriate behaviors with the volunteer group.

Role Play 3: Getting the Job Done
Ask the four volunteers to discuss this question with you: Who would you invite to dinner if you could invite anyone in the world? As you sit with the group, model inappropriate behaviors for a minute or two: Don't ask anyone for help, and don't offer help. Disagree with someone in a personal, negative way. Continually try to change the subject. Talk about a recent campus disruption. Stop, and ask the class: What behaviors were inappropriate? How did group members feel about your behavior? How did the behaviors stand in the way of getting the job done? What can be done to help group members stay on task? After the discussion, reveal Cooperative Skills 8 through 10, and carefully discuss each.

8. Be helpful and assist each other. Point out that there will be interdependence in groupwork activities, and mutual assistance will be needed. Tell students that it is not okay for them to stop working if their part of the task is complete until they have offered assistance to all other group members.

9. Disagree in an agreeable way. Tell students that you expect them to disagree during groupwork activities; disagreement is a normal part of problem solving. Explain that you want the disagreement to stay on an academic level and not become personal. Point out constructive ways to disagree without putting down another's ideas or intellect. For example, group members might repeat an idea they disagree with and then politely give their own idea. Or they might acknowledge the other person's idea by saying: That's one possible approach, but here's another I think we should consider.

At the end of the discussion, role-play the appropriate behaviors with the volunteer group.

10. Stay on task. Remind students that groupwork time is not a social hour, but a time for serious academic work.

When Teach cooperative skills before students begin working in groups. You can teach these skills over several class sessions.

"I learned a lot about working with other people because usually I am rude and say what comes to mind, but I have realized that way hurts a lot of people."
High School Student

Reinforcing Cooperative Skills with Younger Students

In middle school and in some high school classes, be explicit when you teach cooperative skills.

For example, here is how to teach Cooperative Skill 7 to younger students.

1. **Name the behavior.** On the chalkboard, overhead projector, a large piece of butcher paper, or tagboard, write: Use positive comments, encourage, and express appreciation.

2. **Demonstrate the behavior.** Have three volunteers join you in the middle of the class. Ask the group to generate a list of the ten biggest concerns in the United States today. Encourage everyone to participate, and praise group members who come up with good ideas.

3. **Define the behavior.** Below the heading: Use positive comments, encourage, and express appreciation, make a T chart with two columns, Looks Like and Sounds Like. Ask students to identify actions you took and words you said that were positive, encouraging, and appreciative, and list them on the chart. Here are possible entries:

   Looks Like Made eye contact; leaned forward; smiled; nodded head; gave "thumbs-up" sign; gave "high-five" to group member.

   Sounds Like Great idea!; Right!; Say that again so everyone can hear; Thanks; Do you have any other good ideas?

4. **Practice.** Once students have clearly defined the behavior, give them a simple discussion task and allow them to practice in groups. Circulate throughout the room and observe their interaction.

5. **Process the students' experience.** This is where the most lasting learning takes place. Allow students to share their experiences before you comment on what you observed. Ask: How did you feel when your group members used positive comments toward you? How did it feel to express positive ideas? How did using this skill affect your group's ability to work together? Why do you think this is an important cooperative skill?

This five-step process can be used for teaching any of the cooperative skills. Observe your students, and assess their cooperative ability. You may want to reserve this process for the more difficult skills, like Listen to others and take turns giving ideas, or Disagree in an agreeable way.

© Addison-Wesley Publishing Company, Inc.

"I like working in groups when people are friendly and help me."
Middle School Student

History Alive!

Step 7 — Form heterogeneous groups.

Rationale If students are properly placed in heterogeneous groups, several common classroom dilemmas can be solved. First, you are exposing all students to high-level content because they can use one another as resources. Second, you are breaking social cliques and fostering intercultural understanding. Third, you are giving students the skills they will eventually need in order to work with different kinds of people in college, the workplace, and the community.

What to Do Whether you are creating groups of two, three, four, or five, each should be balanced in gender, ethnicity, intelligence (as defined by Howard Gardner), and social group. Keep in mind that your ability to create smooth, functioning groups will improve with each groupwork activity.

Plan to spend about twenty minutes forming heterogeneous groups for each of your classes. Balancing groups in terms of gender and ethnicity is relatively easy. And, after having students together for a short while, you will have an idea of the social circles that exist. The most challenging variable is determining predominant intelligences. The best way is through careful observation throughout the school year. To get a rough idea of your students' cognitive strengths, however, give the simple diagnostic "Where Does Your True Intelligence Lie?" (see p. 13). Use the results, coupled with your observations, to balance groups by cognitive ability.

Depending on the success of the groups you create, you may want to have students remain in the same group for several activities. Or you may want to switch groups to give students a change of pace or to try to make more effective groups. Be aware that each time students move into new groups, group rapport will have to be rebuilt.

When During the third, fourth, or fifth week, and after you have completed steps 1 through 6. You will need to have some knowledge of your students to assess how to group them.

Step 8 — Allow newly formed groups to engage in team-building activities to make students feel comfortable working together and to build group cohesion.

Rationale Before students can effectively engage in curricular groupwork activities, they must feel comfortable with their group members and believe in the value of teamwork. It is imperative that team-building activities—exercises designed to create a more comfortable, cohesive group environment—precede groupwork tasks. The investment in time—ten minutes or a class period—pays off in opportunities for students to interact safely, to get a feel for the interpersonal dynamics within the group, to break social tension, to value teamwork, and to feel at ease working together.

What to Do Once you have created heterogeneous groups and have taught students how to move into groups, you are ready to have students join their group. Follow this procedure:

1. Tell students they will have three minutes to move into their groups. Remind them to break tension and be friendly, to learn and use names, to arrange desks properly, and to use positive

---

They're Only Human

Forming heterogeneous groups is an imperfect science. Expect that some groups may not work as well together as others.

body language. Once students have formed their groups, explain that will be doing a team-building activity designed to enhance their appreciation of teamwork and to make them feel more comfortable with their group members.

2. Give each student a copy of "Lost on the Moon" (see p. 140). Go over the directions and clarify any questions. Emphasize that students are to devise answers to Phase 1 entirely on their own and that there should be no talking until they have all completed their individual ranks. This should take four to six minutes.

3. Now allow groups to begin working on Phase 2, the team's rank. Encourage students to use the Cooperative Skills while coming up with a group solution. (You may want to post the Skills or project them on the overhead.) As students exchange probable solutions, there may be heated discussion. That is okay. If students within a group cannot agree, remind them of the directions: they are to decide the ranks that "best satisfy" all members. Expect that some groups will finish within ten minutes, while others may take significantly longer.

4. After all groups have completed Phase 2, read NASA's ranks while students write them in the correct column. Explain NASA's rationale for each rank. Have students compute the error points for individual and group ranks by finding the absolute difference (disregarding plus and minus signs) between each pair of numbers. In almost all cases, the total number of error points will be significantly lower for the group ranks than for the individual ranks, supporting the notion that teamwork is valuable.

Answers to Lost on the Moon

Item	NASA's Rank	Explanation
A	15	The moon has no oxygen to sustain a flame; matches are virtually worthless.
B	4	An efficient means of supplying energy requirements.
C	6	Useful for scaling cliffs and helping the injured.
D	8	Offers protection from the sun.
E	13	Not needed on the lighted side, and won't work on the dark side.
F	11	A possible means of self-propulsion.
G	12	A bulkier duplication of food concentrate.
H	1	The most pressing survival need.
I	3	The primary means of navigation.
J	9	The CO_2 bottle in the raft may be used for propulsion.
K	14	The moon's magnetic field is not polarized; a magnetic compass is worthless for navigation.
L	2	Replacement for the tremendous liquid loss that will occur on the light side.
M	10	Will be needed for use as a distress signal when the mother ship is sighted.
N	7	Vitamins, medicines, etc., are injected with needles that fit a special aperture in the space suits.
O	5	Needed for communication with mother ship.

Lost on the Moon

Your spaceship has just crash-landed on the light side of the moon. You were scheduled to rendezvous with a mother ship 200 km away on the surface of the moon, but the rough landing has ruined your ship and destroyed all equipment on board, except for the 15 items listed below.

Your crew's survival depends on reaching the mother ship, so you must choose the most critical items for the 200-km trip. Your task is to rank the 15 items in terms of their importance for survival. Place 1 by the most important item, 2 by the second most important, and so on through 15, the least important.

You will rank these items twice. First you will rank them on your own (Phase 1), and then you will consult with your group and rank them again (Phase 2). Share your individual solutions and reach a consensus ranking for each of the 15 items that best satisfies all group members. NASA experts have determined the best solution; their answers will be revealed later.

Item	Phase 1 Your Rank	Error Points	Phase 2 Team Rank	Error Points	NASA's Rank
A. Box of matches					
B. Food concentrate					
C. Fifty feet of nylon rope					
D. Parachute silk					
E. Solar-powered portable heating unit					
F. Two .45-caliber pistols					
G. One case of dehydrated milk					
H. Two 100-pound tanks of oxygen					
I. Stellar map of moon's constellation					
J. Self-inflating life raft					
K. Magnetic compass					
L. Five gallons of water					
M. Signal flares					
N. First-aid kit with injection needles					
O. Solar-powered FM receiver-transmitter					
Total					

5. Hold a class discussion that centers on these questions: Through which process—individual or group—were your answers more accurate? To what do you attribute this? In what ways can working together be beneficial? How did the group interact? Which of the Cooperative Skills did your group employ? Which did you not use? Why? Do you feel more or less comfortable in your group after having done this exercise? What contributed to your increased comfort level? What made you less comfortable?

In most cases, this exercise will allow students to experience the value of teamwork and to feel more comfortable within the group. If, based on your observations and the discussion after the activity, you feel that students are relatively comfortable with their group and that groups are ready to take on a curricular task, your team-building is complete. Some behaviors that signal students are ready to begin curricular work are

- relaxed body language
- friendly facial expressions
- laughter
- interaction that includes all group members
- prolonged discussion

There are two circumstances when you will need team-building activities beyond "Lost on the Moon." First, if "Lost on the Moon" was not effective in building cohesive groups, you may need to do additional team-building. Second, as you change groups during the year, you will need other team-building activities to create cohesion in the new groups.

What follows is a list of other team-building activities that are quick (five to ten minutes), simple, and fun. Remind students that during the activity, each student will have the opportunity to contribute ideas, all group members should listen carefully to the speaker, everyone in the group should show interest in what is being said, and students should ask clarifying questions after the speaker has responded.

Finish That Thought Ask students to discuss one of the following ideas. These are simple, non-academic ideas that will give them something interesting to discuss to ease the tension of working together. Remind students to use their best listening skills as each student responds to the question.

- If I had $1,000,000 I would . . .
- The accomplishment of which I am most proud is . . .
- The most embarrassing thing that ever happened to me was . . .
- Ten years from now I will . . .
- If I were principal of this school for a day, I would . . .
- The car I most would like to have is a . . .
- If I were preparing for my last meal, I'd have . . .
- The discussion I have most often with my family is . . .
- If you walked into my room at home, you'd see . . .
- If I could invite any person over for dinner, I would invite . . .

"I work better after I have had a chance to get to know the people in my group."
Middle School Student

History Alive!

Group Handshake Have groups develop a group handshake and share it with the class. This is a special way for two students to shake hands to show they belong to a particular group. This quick kinesthetic task will help bring students together and ease tension.

Team Logo Pass out pieces of butcher paper and have each group design a logo using words, symbols, drawings, and color. The logos should reflect the interests and personalities of group members. Have group share their logos with the class.

Human Statues Give each group a different object to recreate with their bodies, such as a tree, computer, car, table, bicycle, slide, octopus, elephant, or airplane. You may want to provide bonus points to those groups who can physically recreate their object so well that it is immediately identifiable to the class.

When Use team-building activities when students are embarking on their first formal groupwork activity, usually during the third, fourth, or fifth week of class. Also, use them whenever you form new groups.

Step 9 Allow students to engage in groupwork activities without unnecessary interventions by you.

Rationale One of the main functions of groupwork tasks is to allow students to grapple with difficult historical issues and to learn problem-solving skills. Often, teachers are too quick to intervene when students appear stuck. Instead, allow students to struggle and perhaps even fail at a task, provided that the class debriefs the process to ascertain what worked and what did not.

"I feel like every student in here is allowed to express his or her beliefs freely, regardless of others' or the teacher's opinions. Respect is always guaranteed and enforced."
High School Student

What to Do Once students begin to work on a groupwork task, use your time to ensure on-task behavior, to record group progress for evaluation, and to note the various processes groups are using. Curb impulses to control group interaction; don't hover around the groups and engage in problem solving. If students ask for substantive help, try to help them figure out how to solve the issue among themselves. Only accept "team questions," questions for which all group members have their hands in the air.

The critical role for you comes after students have finished the groupwork activity. Then it's time for you to lead a discussion focusing on the group process, a process essential to continue building cooperative skill effectiveness—not just in groupwork, but in daily classroom interaction. Center your discussion around these questions: How did your group interact? Which of the Cooperative Skills were exhibited the most? Which were exhibited the least? What did your group do well? What could it have improved upon? If another group of students were to do this same activity, what suggestions would you make?

When Any time students are engaged in groupwork activities.

Step 10 Discuss the three premises behind the *History Alive!* program with your students.

Rationale Students can become even more active and informed learners if you explain to them the rationale behind your teaching. Students are fascinated and appreciative (especially after they have experienced several activities) when they discover why you are teaching a certain way. The information will help them better understand you, the class, and their own learning styles so that they can benefit even more from this approach.

What to Do After you have finished your first or second unit, reveal to students to the three premises of the *History Alive!* approach (as discussed in Chapter 1). This is critical for two reasons. It informs students of the theories that guide what they have been experiencing in class, thus giving them a clearer understanding of the rationale behind the curriculum. More importantly, it validates the academic worth of all class members by pointing out that individuals have different abilities and unique talents, which, when properly integrated, allows diverse learners to learn together.

Make "Premises of the Program" into an overhead transparency and project it. Discuss each premise with your students, and have them give examples of ways in which each premise has been acknowledged and addressed in your class.

When Reveal this after students have had at least four weeks' experience with the *History Alive!* approach.

> *"This class is centered around the students' needs. Everything is at a personal, comfortable level so all students can learn."*
> **High School Student**

Premises of the Program

Premise 1: Students have different learning styles.

"To my mind, a human intellectual competence must entail a set of skills of problem solving and also entail the potential for finding or creating problems."[3]
—Howard Gardner, Harvard University Neuropsychologist

Gardner's list of multiple intelligences:
- linguistic
- logical-mathematical
- visual-spatial
- body-kinesthetic
- musical-rhythmic
- intrapersonal
- interpersonal

Premise 2: Cooperative interaction increases learning and improves social skills.

"Groupwork is an effective technique for achieving certain kinds of intellectual and social learning goals. It is a superior technique for conceptual learning, for creative problem solving, and for increasing oral language proficiency."[4]
—Elizabeth Cohen, Professor of Sociology and Education at Stanford University

Premise 3: All students can learn.

"Any subject can be taught effectively in some intellectually honest form to any child at any stage of development. Through a spiral curriculum students learn progressively more difficult concepts through step-by-step self-discovery."[5]
—Jerome Bruner

© Addison-Wesley Publishing Company, Inc.

CHAPTER 8

Interactive Student Notebooks

Interactive Student Notebooks allow students to record information about history in an engaging way. As students learn new ideas, they use several types of writing and innovative graphic techniques to record them. They then *do something* with those ideas, such as transforming written concepts into visuals, finding the main point of a political cartoon, and organizing historical events into a topical net. This process encourages students to use their critical-thinking skills to organize and process information. As a result, **students become more creative, more independent thinkers.**

The first time you see an Interactive Student Notebook, you will notice colorful and varied expression. Words and diagrams, bullets and arrows, ink and pencil, a multitude of colors, and highlighting are all presented in a unique, personal style. Traditional student notebooks may work for motivated students with strong linguistic skills, but they do not serve students who have other learning styles. In Interactive Student Notebooks, key ideas are underlined in color or highlighted; Venn diagrams show relationships; cartoon sketches show people and events; time lines illustrate chronology; indentations and bullets indicate subordination; arrows show cause-and-effect relationships. Students develop graphic thinking skills, and those who were alienated in the conventional classroom are motivated to understand and to express their ideas.

To create Interactive Student Notebooks, students must bring these materials to class each day:

- Their $8\frac{1}{2}$-by-11-inch spiral-bound notebook, with at least one hundred pages
- A pen
- A pencil with an eraser
- Two felt-tip pens of different colors

"My notebook is like a carousel because it's colorful, organized, and fun."
High School Student

A Simple Spiral Does It All

A spiral-bound notebook is more effective than any other type—three-ring binders, folders, gummed or perforated notebooks—because it is more durable, the pages stay in the proper sequence, and it lays flat for easy left-side, right-side use.

"The notebooks were very helpful because writing is a form of learning. I personally didn't like writing in my notebook, because I hate notes. But it definitely helped."
High School Student

History Alive!

- Two highlighters of different colors
- A container for all of these (purse, backpack, vinyl packet)

Tell students that these additional materials would be helpful:

- A variety of colored pens
- Several more highlighters
- A small pair of scissors
- Rubber cement or a glue stick

Give students three or four days to purchase these materials. For students with limited financial resources, keep materials in the classroom or use school funds to help these students purchase them.

Have students create a title page on the first page of the notebook by writing the name of the course in large, colorful letters. At the bottom of the page, they can add their name and the class period. Encourage them to embellish this page with a border and a small diagram or two. For each new unit, have students write the title of the unit on a right-hand page. You might want to require students to find a picture or to draw an illustration on the left-hand page that represents a theme of the unit. Here are additional ideas that encourage students to create notebooks that are visually and graphically appealing.

- Model a variety of visual techniques in the notes your require students to take. You might use an outline one day, a spectrum the next, and a matrix the next.
- Teach students to use color to highlight meaning, not just as decoration.
- Put the title and date for each activity on the board, and have students copy and highlight them.
- Have students look at each others' notebooks for alternative graphic approaches.
- Encourage students to leave blank spaces throughout their notebooks for pasting in relevant clippings and cartoons and for adding comments when they review for tests.

Right-side, Left-side Orientation

Interactive Student Notebooks encourage students to record notes in an organized, logical fashion and to work with and process the information in ways that help them better understand history. The right side of the notebook—the "input" side—is used for recording class notes, discussion notes, and reading notes. Typically, all "testable" information is found here. Students structure notes so that key ideas and concepts are clear and supported by examples.

The left side—the "output" side—is primarily used for processing new ideas. Students work out an understanding of new material by using illustrations, diagrams, flow charts, poetry, colors, matrices, cartoons, and the like. Students explore their opinions and clarify their values on controversial issues, wonder "what if" in hypothetical situations, and ask questions about

> **The left side of the notebook is used primarily for students to process new ideas. Here students are encouraged to:**
>
> - "Work out" an understanding of new material — like information presented in an Interactive Slide Lecture — by using illustrations, diagrams, flow charts, poetry, colors, matrices, cartoons, songs and the like.
>
> - Explore their options and clarify their values on controversial issues, wonder "what if" in hypothetical situations, and ask questions about new ideas.
>
> - Demonstrate their creativity, curiosity, and analysis as they encounter new material.
>
> - Express their feelings and reactions to activities — like Experiential Exercises — which tap into intrapersonal learning.
>
> - Review what they have learned, and preview what they will learn. By doing so, students are encouraged to always try to see how individual lessons fit into the larger context of a unit.
>
> **The right side of the notebook is used for recording class notes, discussion notes, and reading notes.**
>
> - Typically, all "testable" information is found here. As students take notes, they should structure them so that key ideas and concepts are clear and supported by examples from lectures, discussions, and readings.
>
> - This side will also be a place for students to state refined conclusions and personal positions. These conclusions will be the polished versions of ideas students grappled with on the left side of the notebook.

The division of the Interactive Student Notebook into right and left sides is critical to student learning.

Save the Good Ones

If some students produce particularly good notebooks, ask at the end of each year if you may keep them to use as models for your students the next year.

---

new ideas. They also express their feelings and reactions to activities that tap into intrapersonal learning. And they review what they have learned and preview what they will learn. By doing so, students are encouraged to see how individual lessons fit into the larger context of a unit.

- It stresses that writing down lecture notes does not mean students have learned the information. They must actively *do* something with the information before they internalize it.
- It clearly indicates which ideas are the teacher's and which are the student's. *Everything* on the left is the student's.
- It gives students permission to be playful and experimental since they know the left side is their page and they will not be interfering with class notes.
- It can serve as an immediate and powerful reminder to you. Blank left-hand pages will indicate that you are providing too much information without time for students to process the material. If you notice many blank left-hand pages, you need to restructure the activity to get students actively engaged.

A notebook with this left-side, right-side orientation engages students in learning history for several reasons.

■ **Students use both their visual and linguistic intelligence.** In these notebooks, students approach understanding in many ways. As they grapple with new ideas, they will use several types of writing and several graphic techniques. The left side allows visual learners to use their best medium to explore and to share ideas, and encourages nonvisual learners to become more proficient with graphic approaches in a nonthreatening way. Likewise, both types of learners will work with their writing skills. All students benefit from this two-pronged approach.

History Alive!

> "Students like that the notebooks allow them the freedom and creativity to express themselves in a variety of ways. Parents continually tell me that they think it's fantastic that kids are paying attention to current events, relating them to history, and writing about it in their notebooks."
>
> *Diane Gill,*
> *High School Teacher*

Students use the right side of the notebook to record factual information and the left side to work out their understanding of that information.

■ **Note-taking becomes an active process.** These notebook reach out to students, inviting them to become engaged in their learning. Students will devote a little time to passively record ideas from a lecture or the board, but most of the time they are *doing* something with ideas: putting them into their own words, searching for implications or assumptions, transforming words into visuals, finding the main point of a political cartoon. This is especially true on the left side of the notebook, which is reserved for the students' active exploration of the ideas of the course.

■ **Students' creativity is unleashed.** Short-answer questions and fill-in-the-blanks are not found in these notebooks. Students might write a letter to a person in the past, create an anti-slavery political cartoon for publication during the Civil War, or write a dialogue between a slave owner and a slave. All of these activities require students to create a whole product rather than fragmented, isolated products.

■ **Notebooks help students to systematically organize as they learn.** Encourage students to use their notebooks to record ideas about every activity they engage in during a unit. Have them use organizational techniques—topic headings, colored highlights, different writing styles—to synthesize historical concepts.

■ **Notebooks become a portfolio of individual learning.** These personal, creative notebooks become a record of each student's growth. Teachers, students, and even families can review a student's progress in writing, graphic, recording, and organization skills.

> "Notebooks help me on the tests and the way my teacher does it, it is easy to understand."
>
> *Middle School Student*

Chapter 8

The Right Side

The right-hand side of the notebook is reserved for students to input information, whether from you, a movie, an author, or other students. Show your students how to take neat, thorough, organized notes so that they can easily understand them later. Encourage them to differentiate key ideas from supporting ideas. And teach them how to identify key ideas and develop graphic devices to indicate those ideas, be it during a lecture, a class discussion, or a reading assignment.

To illustrate this approach, let's look at two styles of note taking on the topic of imperialism. First, look at the following notes, which are neat and complete but have no graphic indications of importance.

> Imperialism is controlling other people by not allowing them to make their own decisions. This can be military, economic or political imperialism. An example is the Philippines. Expansionism is the outward movement of a people that may displace other people, like our frontier. Some people don't like imperialism because we need to solve our own problems first. It violates our Declaration of Independence and it may be racist. It may have economic benefits. It spreads Christianity. It also helps us become a world power.

This student had trouble focusing on the main idea. Let's see how this same lecture would be represented with graphic notes indicating the main ideas.

> Imperialism vs. Expansionism
> <u>Imperialism</u>: Controlling other peoples and not allowing them to make their own decisions. <u>Formal</u>: Military   <u>Informal</u>: Economic or political
>   EXAMPLE: Philippines
> <u>Expansionism</u>: The outward movement of a people, which may displace other peoples.
>   EXAMPLE: The American Frontier
>   Arguments against Imperialism
>   • We need to solve our own problems first
>   • Violates Declaration of Independence
>   • Often racist (white vs. black, white vs. Asian)
>   Arguments for Imperialism
>   • Economic benefits for America
>   • Spreads Christianity
>   • Spreads American civilization
>   • Helps us become world power

"My notebook is like an encyclopedia because I can look up any information that I took notes on quickly and easily."
High School Student

History Alive!

The first example doesn't clearly indicate whether expansionism is an example of imperialism or something different. Nor does it boldly delineate arguments for and against imperialism. In the second example, these key ideas are very clear because several graphic techniques were used to indicate subordination:

- Size of letters
- Boldness of letters
- Capital letters
- Indentations
- Underlining
- Bullets

Encourage students to use color pens and highlighters. They can write key words in color, underline them with other colors, and put bullets or numbers in color as well. They can use highlighters to draw attention to key concepts and organizing ideas. They can make colored drawings and diagrams.

Not only will graphic techniques help all students remember their notes, but they will also help you reach out to those students who are predominantly visual learners. When you plan a presentation, use different graphic approaches to organize it. This adds variety to the students' notebooks and helps present and clarify ideas for many students.

Notes from reading should employ graphic and organizational elements. Encourage students to record impressions from readings—textbook, primary source, periodical, literature—in a variety of ways. While there are times

> *"Notebooks were very useful. They helped me organize my thoughts, which is usually very difficult for me."*
> **Middle School Student**

Showcase Great Notes

When teaching students how to take good class notes, make an overhead transparency of a particularly good student sample and share it with the class.

Students use the teacher's outline as a basis for their notes on the right side of their notebooks.

Chapter 8

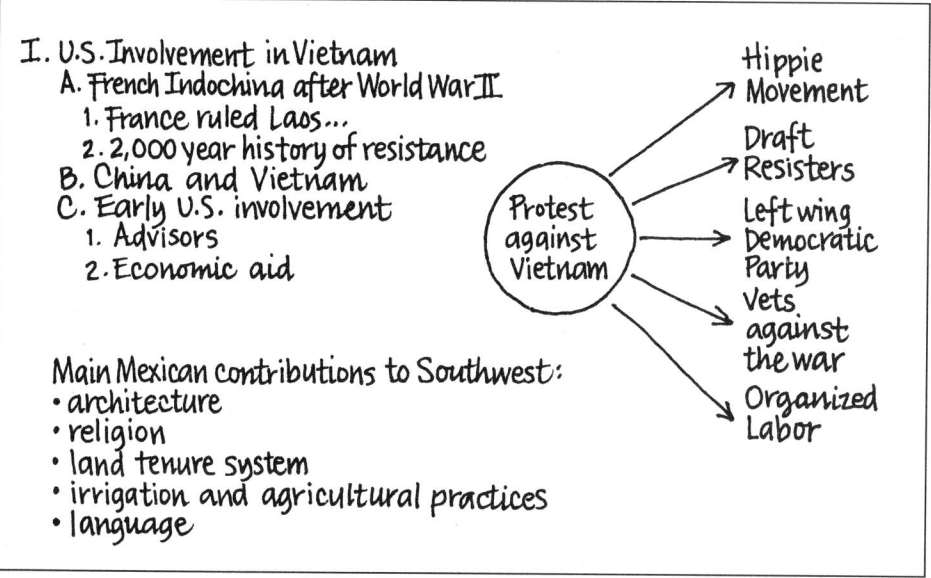

Use a variety of graphic presentations when you model note-taking. Encourage students to highlight main ideas and new vocabulary words in their notes with colored markers. This makes it easier for them to quickly review their notes.

when traditional outline notes are best for summarizing, other forms are often more appropriate. For example, you might have students respond to a reading by

- using one concise sentence to state the author's main point
- stating the best evidence the author uses to support his or her point
- writing a paragraph that summarizes the narrative of a historical reading
- giving students the main point of a reading and then having them explain several key ideas the writer uses to support it
- listing three new ideas from the reading and connecting them with three ideas introduced in class
- responding to questions you've prepared that are crafted to focus on the main points of the reading

The Left Side

The left side of the Interactive Student Notebook allows students to process, question, and wrestle with the new ideas and information they encounter. Four types of entries can help students make the most of the left side: Reviewing and Previewing, Working It Out, Personal Response, and Here I Stand.

Reviewing and Previewing

Reviewing and Previewing, RAP, is used mostly as a transition or sponge activity. Use RAPs as many as two or three times a week to help students make connections between what they have learned and what they will

"The notebook totally changed the way I teach. It gives me limitless ways to keep the students involved."
Jim Smith,
High School Teacher

What's the Rap?

RAPs are transition activities that make connections between what has been learned and what will be learned.

History Alive!

learn. During a RAP, students write or draw for two or three minutes in response to a question or statement that either helps them review the content of a past lesson or preview what is ahead. Then, a handful of students are called on to share their responses with the class. In doing so, they either review key ideas from the previous day's lesson or build anticipation for the upcoming topic.

You can use RAPs to begin class with a short review of what happened the previous day. This will help students remember key ideas they have already studied and relate them to the current lesson. You may want to challenge students to combine visual elements with their written work. Here are examples of RAPs that *preview* new topics.

- List three unanswered questions you have about the Vietnam War.
- Finish this idea: As I understand it, the Supreme Court's job is . . .
- List three things you know about the Holocaust.
- Complete this thought: A war is justified when . . .
- What is the purpose of a government?
- "Might makes right." Do you agree with this statement? Explain.

Here are examples of RAPs that *review* what has been taught.

- List five reasons why immigrants came to the United States.
- In one concise paragraph, explain five causes of the French Revolution.
- Choose five words or phrases that best describe the actions of a major civil-rights leader.
- List three differences between the empires of Ghana and Mali.
- List three key reasons for the fall of the Roman Empire.
- Finish this idea: The chief concerns of the women at the Seneca Falls Convention were . . .
- The New Deal was like a _____ . Complete this sentence, draw an illustration of your metaphor, and briefly explain it.

Here are other ideas for RAPs.

- Draw a rough map on the board. Have students copy in into their notebooks and locate three or four places that have been studied so far. Then have them use their geographical knowledge to make some predictions about the topic that will be covered in class today. You might use this RAP to introduce a lesson on the frontier.
- Have students think of a time when they felt taken advantage of and wanted revenge. Have them write a few sentences about what happened, how they felt, and what they ended up doing. Encourage them to represent this with a drawing. Use this to introduce a lesson, for example, on the Treaty of Versailles.
- Put four key terms on the board that have been studied so far. Have students use them in a short paragraph that shows what they mean and how they relate to each other. They may include an illustration if they choose. Then introduce the key term for

today, and have students predict its meaning and how it relates to other key terms. This technique might work well for lessons on political or economic terms.

- On the board, draw a rough sketch of a dog, along with the names of two leaders from history that were studied earlier in the unit. Ask students to decide what kind of dog each of these leaders were and to explain why. Encourage them to sketch each dog and person. Finally, pick a type of dog for the person they will be studying today. Have students predict some of the characteristics of the person given the type of dog. Use this to introduce any lesson on important leaders.

Working It Out

As active learners, students must paraphrase, criticize, extend, apply, and wrestle with new information. Without this active involvement, most students will only superficially understand new ideas. Students use Working It Outs in class or as homework to represent new ideas in meaningful and comprehensible ways: they take large bodies of notes or difficult concepts and "work out" meanings on the left side of their notebooks. After a movie, Interactive Slide Lecture, reading, or class discussion, students review the notes on the right side and reorganize them into a new format they understand and find memorable. They also help students to clarify difficult concepts, such as Manifest Destiny, federalism, and colonialism. See the example on page 154 for possible formats.

You may want to check on understanding of new material by asking students to select some type of Working It Out—such as a spectrum, illustration, caricature, topical net, Venn diagram, or matrix—to complete. Display some examples of Working It Outs to help them get started. Once students understand the range of choices they have in an open-ended Working It Out assignment, they will be free to choose the option with which they are most comfortable.

In some cases, you may want to structure an activity; for example, you might want to work on a specific skill, such as evaluating evidence. A structured Working It Out will require all students to practice the same skill, and since everyone is solving the same problem, sharing ideas will be easier and more interesting. And a structured Working It Out lends itself to groupwork: two, three, or four students can cooperate to solve a common problem or work on a shared activity. Here are some examples of structured Working It Outs.

- **Ask students to summarize information in a single sentence.** You might ask students to "summarize the main point of today's lesson in one excellent sentence," or to "use only one sentence to state your position about affirmative action and give one supporting reason."

- **Have students create spoke diagrams that make sense of information they have just received.** A spoke diagram is a drawing with a central idea in the middle around which supporting ideas radiate. For example, ask

"Working It Outs allow me to take what the teacher has said and write it, draw it, or diagram it in a way that makes sense to me. After I do this, I really understand what we did in class."
High School Student

Making the Private Public

Structure a time for students to share their notebooks with one another so they can appreciate how many different ways there are to create and work out ideas.

History Alive!

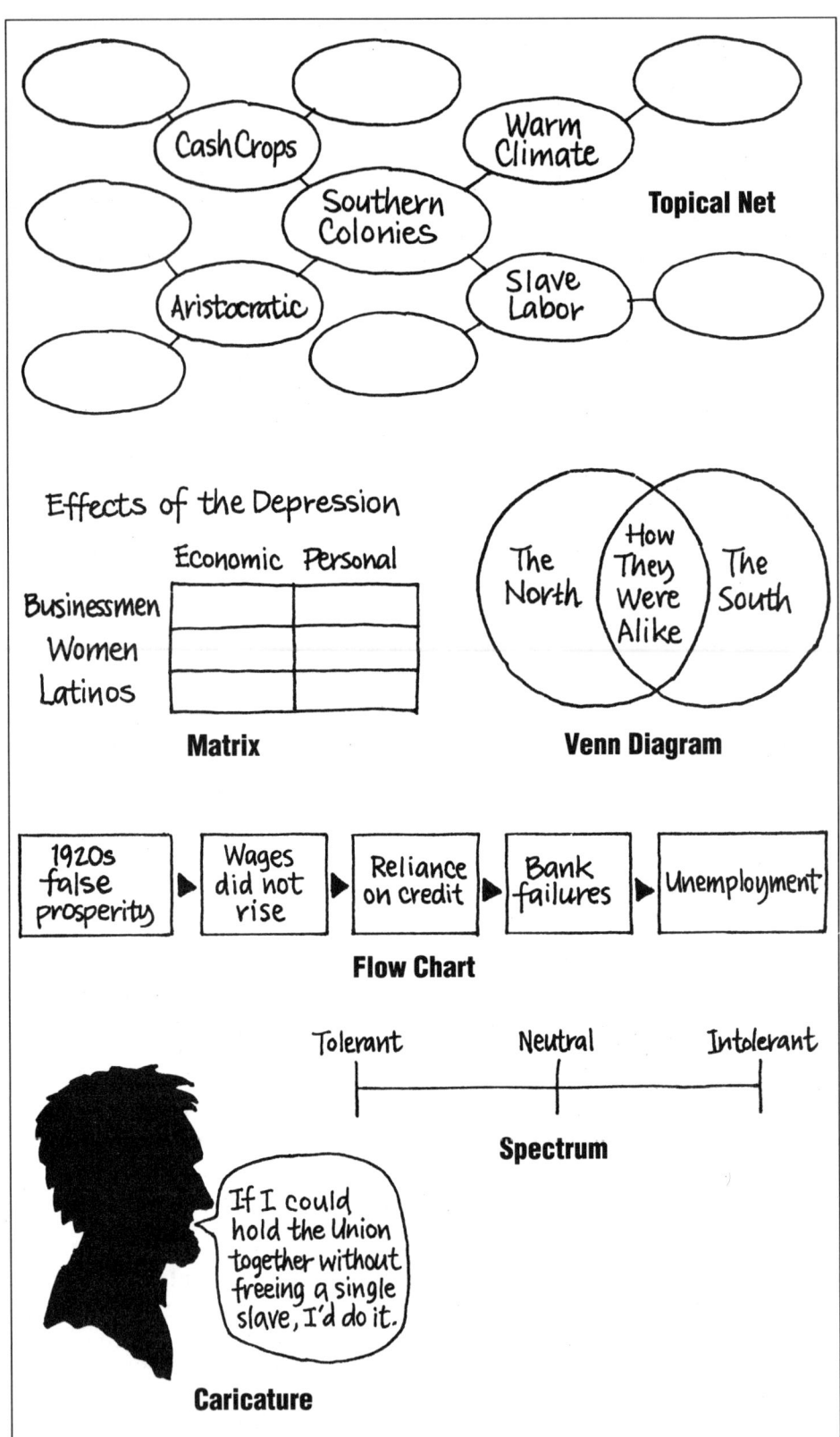

Students represent key concepts with a variety of graphics that help them understand and remember them.

students to "create a spoke diagram of the homework you read tonight and highlight those ideas for which you need more information." Or tell students to "create a spoke diagram that accurately represents the discussion we just had. Represent each basic point of view with a different color."

- **Give students a metaphor to examine.** For example, after a discussion of immigration from Europe, you might ask students: "How was the New World like a magnet for the Europeans? Find four important similarities and two important differences." Or during a unit on the Soviet Union, you might ask students: "We have just been reading and talking about Lenin. List different metaphors that represent his actions and his personality. Which is the best metaphor? Why?"

- **Challenge students to answer What if? questions.** During a unit on the civil-rights movement, for example, ask students to finish this idea: "If Martin Luther King and Malcolm X had not been assassinated, I think the course of history would have been altered in these ways: . . ." After an activity on the Electoral College, ask students: "Brainstorm some plusses and minuses if we were to start a computerized voting system with a 'voting computer' in each house."

Personal Response

Personal Responses are either prompted by you or initiated by students when they want to express an idea or to ask a question about the content. Personal Responses allow students to explore their feelings, to voice their opinions, or to reflect on how a topic touches their own lives. They should be open-ended, enabling the students to react individually to new ideas. Here are some examples.

Finish this idea:

- The most compelling argument made by isolationists was . . .
- What struck me most during my interview with a recent immigrant was . . .
- I like the art of the Renaissance period more/less than medieval art because . . .
- To me, the most significant difference between feudal Europe and feudal Japan was . . .
- If I had been drafted during the Vietnam War, I would have _____ because . . .
- From my point of view, the most horrible thing about slavery was . . ."
- Had I voted in 1960, I would have cast my vote for _____ because . . .

Here I Stand

Here I Stands allow students to state conclusions and personal positions on issues. Unlike Personal Responses, their intent is for students to produce precise and polished prose on ideas they have been grappling with throughout a unit. These conclusive statements should demonstrate a relative mastery of the content and express a well-supported opinion. Usually, Here I Stands

---

Use Them Often

Use Working It Outs frequently, so your students will gain a deeper understanding of history. This kind of active learning is the most crucial part of the Interactive Student Notebook.

"The notebook allows me to express my opinions about what we are learning. I usually don't get to do that in my other classes."
Middle School Student

History Alive!

take up to a page or more. Occasionally, you may want to have students express their views in a few carefully crafted sentences. Here are some positions on issues on which students might base a Here I Stand.

- Did the Progressives go far enough in their reform?
- The federal government should provide more aid to the poor. Do you agree or disagree? Explain.
- Manifest Destiny was justified. Do you agree or disagree? Explain.
- The Industrial Revolution improved life for the working class. Do you agree or disagree? Explain.
- Were the Russians better off under the Czar or Stalin? Explain.
- Government in the United States is of the people, by the people, and for the people. Do you agree or disagree? Explain.
- For the last three days, we have been examining the Vietnam War. In three sentences, state your position on this controversial war.
- Whose policies were better for America, Hamilton's or Jefferson's? Why?
- Latin America was better off before the Spaniards arrived. Do you agree or disagree? Explain.

The Extras: Student-Initiated Entries

Class notes, RAPs, Working It Outs, Here I Stands, and some Personal Responses are structured and shaped by you. Once students begin to feel comfortable with the interactive notebook system, they are ready to explore ideas on their own, to raise questions of interest to them, and to make connections between current events and the history they are learning. Any entries students make on their own should be applauded. Here are some ideas to help your students take the creative visual and linguistic techniques they have learned to create their own notebook entries.

1. Newspaper clippings and political cartoons. This is the easiest way to spice up a notebook. Encourage your students to scour magazines and newspapers to find connections between current events and what is being studied in class. Ideally, students will paste these clippings or political cartoons into the notebook in proximity to the material to which they relate. A cartoon about power corrupting might be pasted across from class notes on Napoleon. Have students write a sentence or two commenting on the connection between the clipping and the class topic. They might also highlight key passages from a newspaper clipping or alter a cartoon to make it more relevant or humorous.

2. Drawings and illustrations. Encourage students to use their artistic talent to graphically annotate class notes wherever and however they want. They might draw small visuals to accompany key ideas, put faces of historic personalities in blank spaces, redraw textbook maps, or create cartoon panels for explaining historical events.

3. Personal Responses. Personal Responses give voice to shy students or students who do not get called upon. Have students open to a blank page, title it Personal Response, and begin writing. Students may write one or two

---

"My notebook is like a security blanket because I can write my thoughts about anything in it and understand them more, which gives me confidence when answering questions."
Middle School Student

"The current events part of the notebook made me want to learn more. I'll tell you, I even started watching the news and explaining things to my mom."
Middle School Student

Chapter 8

Encourage students to search magazines and newspapers for clippings or political cartoons that relate to what is being studied in class.

sentences or an entire page. Encouraging students to personalize what they are learning in class helps them connect with history and promotes more active learning.

Grading Interactive Student Notebooks

An effective system for grading notebooks will keep the task from becoming burdensome and time-consuming. Here are some suggestions to help you manage the load of grading student notebooks so that students can receive regular, helpful feedback.

Daily Evaluation Suggestions

- Check notebooks each day for the first two weeks of the semester. It is imperative that you give immediate feedback in the early stages to determine whether students are using the notebooks correctly and to address any problems immediately.

It Needn't Be a Grading Nightmare!

Don't let the prospect of having to grade a class set of notebooks scare you away from using this technique daily. Recognize that you can't grade everything in each notebook. Develop an evaluation system that is efficient for you and fair to your students.

Notebook Evaluation Sheet   Name _____

Before turning in your notebooks, grade yourself on each of the assignments below, as well as on Visual Appearance and Extras. Grade yourself fairly and honestly; I will grade you as well. I will tell you clearly what I am looking for. Keep in mind that my grade is binding, but if there is a discrepancy, you may politely arrange a time to meet with me to discuss the difference in assessment. After we meet, I reserve the right to change the grade if I made an error in judgment; however, I also reserve the right to stick by my original grade.

Notebook Entry	Date	Possible Points	Student Assessment	Teacher Assessment
Extras				
Visual Appearance				
Totals				

Student Comments

Teacher Comments

- Walk around the classroom while students are working and give positive comments and helpful suggestions. This is important early in the year, and from time to time throughout the year. Otherwise, students may get careless and the quality of their notebooks will suffer.
- If you have given a Working It Out for homework, look at each notebook at the student's desk and evaluate it using 0 (not done), ✓ (needs work), ÷ (average effort), and + (excellent). Record these in your grade book.
- If you assigned a short writing, have students photocopy it and turn it in for a grade.
- Pass out a model of outstanding notes for a particular lecture or activity. Put students into groups of two and have them evaluate their notebooks according to the model.
- On occasion, allow students to use their reading or class notes to take a quiz. If their notes are good, their grade should reflect this.

Formal Evaluation

At the end of each unit or at the end of a grading period, formally evaluate notebooks. Create a Notebook Evaluation handout (see the example on p. 158) with five columns: Notebook Entry, Date, Possible Points, Student Assessment, and Teacher Assessment. In the Notebook Entry column, list the assignments you want to grade. Have students assess their notebooks before they turn them in to you. This enables them to reflect on their learning and to critically review their notebook entries and organization. The need for self-assessment is discussed fully in Chapter 9.

After students have graded their own notebooks, collect them and grade them yourself. You need not grade every notebook entry for the unit or grading period. Instead, carefully evaluate some of the most important entries, such as Here I Stands or Working It Outs, and spot-check a few of the other assignments, such as RAPs and class notes, for quality and thoroughness.

In addition, assess aesthetic appearance and student-initiated extras. Criteria for aesthetic appearance include neatness, organization, effective use of color, and appropriate use of highlighters. Student-initiated extras include newspaper clippings, illustrations, and unassigned Personal Responses.

"Kids like Interactive Notebooks. Instead of receiving piles of worksheets each day, teachers are getting notebooks complete with a variety of forms of expression—personalized feedback on what students are learning, artwork, graphics, timelines, maps, and song lyrics. As a result there's more learning, more retention, more interest, and more involvement."
Herlinda Belcher,
High School Teacher

CHAPTER 9

Multiple-Ability Assessment

Multiple-ability assessment is designed to allow students of different abilities show what they know and can do. Unlike conventional assessment that emphasizes memorization of factual information, multiple-ability assessment encourages students to use information and concepts in a variety of contexts. A multiple-ability assessment task might challenge students to create a visual metaphor, to record an oral history, to videotape a reenactment of past events, or to prepare a travel brochure for a historic site. In a multiple-ability assessment program, students are assessed both on day-to-day classroom activities and on culminating projects that ask them to demonstrate their mastery of a unit.

There is a truism in assessment circles that says that what you test or assess in the classroom ultimately determines what you get in terms of teaching and learning. According to Dale Carlson, head of the California Assessment Program and President of the National Council on Measurement in Education, "the WYTIWYG principle (What You Test Is What You Get) is as trustworthy as Newton's third law of motion. The implications are obvious: We must make our tests authentic embodiments of our goals; they must represent the kinds of student work we value."[1]

Too often assessment in traditional history classes revolves around worksheet completion, periodic quizzes, and traditional short-answer and multiple-choice tests. Assessment of this sort puts a premium on the memorization and regurgitation of facts. Seldom are students encouraged to demonstrate subject mastery in meaningful ways. As assessment expert Grant Wiggins has observed, social studies tests are "an expedient to check up on whether kids mastered some facts, but [have] nothing to do with the authentic act of mastering historical analysis and information."[2]

By putting so much emphasis on the memorization of facts, traditional tests focus quite narrowly on logical and linguistic intelligences. Students

History Alive!

> "We must overcome the lazy habit of grading and scoring 'on the curve' as a cheap way of setting and upholding standards . . . such scoring insures that, by design, at least half of the student population is always made to feel inept and discouraged about their work, while the other half often has a feeling of achievement that is illusory."[3]
>
> **Grant Wiggins,**
> **Executive Director of Consultants on Learning, Assessment, and School Structure**

who are not strong in these areas are at a disadvantage and often perform poorly. As a result, such tests are neither equitable nor accurate in gauging all students' mastery of a subject.

Multiple-ability assessment emphasizes activities in which students use their different intelligences to demonstrate understanding of content in meaningful ways. This approach is guided by the following beliefs:

■ **Good assessment goes to the heart of essential learning.** The tests and tasks used to evaluate students should focus on the understandings and abilities that matter most, not on what is easy to test.

■ **Good assessment works for all students.** Students come into the classroom with varying abilities, learning styles, work paces, and backgrounds. Assessments must be sufficiently varied and flexible in design to accommodate this diversity. Challenging tasks should to be "scaffolded up" rather than "dumbed down" to make them accessible to all students.

■ **Good assessment encourages rather than demoralizes students.** Assessment activities should help students to identify and reveal their strengths rather than constantly highlight their weaknesses.

■ **Good assessment is based on and communicates clearly stated standards.** Assessment activities should communicate to all students what it means to do something well. Grades should be based on standards students both know and understand, not on arbitrary norms or curves.

Good assessment, such as allowing students to demonstrate their content mastery by publishing a topical newspaper, encourages students.

■ **Good assessment is part of the day-to-day classroom curriculum.** Assessment activities should be an integral part of the curriculum rather than occasional intrusions with no purpose other than to "shake out a grade." If an activity is worth students' time and effort, it should be worth assessing as well.

■ **Good assessment activities are indistinguishable from good learning activities.** Assessment activities should be both educational and engaging. They present students with complex, real-life problems to solve or tasks to complete. Such tasks move students beyond factual recall toward higher, richer levels of knowing, and are more likely to culminate in student products or performances than in answer sheets.

■ **Good assessment fosters the habit of self-assessment.** Assessment activities should encourage students to evaluate their own work critically and to reflect on their own growth and progress over time.

Assessing Day-to-Day Activities

Multiple-ability assessment begins with the assessment of day-to-day activities. Assessing daily activities is important for a number of reasons. For teachers, frequent and ongoing assessment provides timely feedback on what is working for students and what is not. This information is essential for identifying problems in time to make appropriate mid-course corrections.

Making assessment part of everyday activities is equally valuable for students. First, it communicates the message that every activity is important and therefore worth evaluating. Second, it encourages students to apply high standards to all of their work. Third, it helps students to identify their own strengths and weaknesses in a safe, low-stakes setting and to reflect on ways to improve in future efforts.

You can build assessment into almost any activity in two ways. First, when setting up an activity, take time to spell out the standards of excellence students should keep in their mind as they work. You can do this by modeling good work, listing performance criteria, or by asking student to help in defining the standards by which their work should be judged. Second, at the end of an activity, leave time for students to reflect on how well they have met those standards, either by assessing their work individually or in a class debriefing session. Below are additional suggestions for making assessment part of the learning strategies and activities you have read about in this book.

Interactive Student Notebooks

Interactive Student Notebooks are central to daily assessment. Students are continually working in their notebooks, taking notes, doing RAPs, and exploring their ideas in a Working It Out or Here I Stand assignment. Make assessment part of this activity by

> ■ wandering about the classroom while students work on notebook entries, using this time to assist students who are having trouble, to make helpful suggestions, to give positive feedback, and to encourage students to assess their own work.

"When educators talk of assessment, they generally think in terms of documented assessment systems. A completely different level of assessment takes place in the individual student, who is constantly assessing her own work, deciding what is right and wrong, what fits and what does not, what is a 'good enough' job. This self-appraisal is the ultimate locus of all standards."[4]
Ron Berger,
Elementary School Teacher

"It's a common-sense case that says if we value it, we should assess it."[5]
Grant Wiggins

History Alive!

- having students work in pairs to critique each other's work.
- asking students to photocopy and turn in a certain paragraph, map, graph, or drawing for you to evaluate.
- collecting notebooks at regular intervals to evaluate overall quality of the work.

Interactive Slide Lectures

During Interactive Slide Lectures students analyze visual images, take notes on what they hear, and sometimes "step into" an image to act out what they think might be going on. You can assess students' attentiveness and understanding of the material presented in a slide lecture based on

- their answers to slide-lecture questions and participation in Act It Outs.
- the thoroughness of the notes in their notebooks.
- their understanding of the key ideas as demonstrated in a Working It Out assignment.
- their performance on a quiz reviewing the content of the slide lecture.

Social Studies Skill Builders

Immediate assessment and feedback is built into these fast-paced skill activities. As pairs of students present their work to you for evaluation, you may want to assess

- the quality and accuracy of their answers on the student handout and expressed orally to you.
- each student's ability to work effectively and cooperatively with a partner. To encourage this cooperation, have pairs alternate who explains their answers to you as you award points.

Experiential Exercises

Experiential Exercises call on students to react spontaneously and even emotionally to simulated historical moments, events, and situations. For this reason, assessment should be delayed until the debriefing. Once student have discussed their experiences, however, you may want to assess your students based on

- how well they met your behavior standards and learning expectations.
- their responses to questions during the debriefing.
- follow-up activities in which students reflect on what they have learned from the exercise and link that learning to broader historical issues.

"The vitality of thought is in adventure. Ideas won't keep. Something must be done with them."
Alfred North Whitehead

Connect the Past to the Present

The best assessment for Experiential Exercises are follow-up activities that link what was learned to broader historical issues.

Response Groups

Response Groups promote critical thinking by asking students to explore provocative, open-ended questions in small groups and then to summarize their thinking for the class. In assessing this activity, you might choose to emphasize

- participation in group discussions.
- the ability of the presenter to clearly articulate the group's thinking.
- the quality of the responses on student worksheets.
- clarity of thinking in writing activities based on Response Group activities.

Writing for Understanding

Writing for Understanding activities challenge students to process what they have learned and experienced in a fresh way and then to present their ideas effectively using a specific writing genre. In assessing this activity you may want to emphasize both the writing process and the final product by looking at each student's

- participation in pre-writing activities and peer response groups.
- incorporation of peer and teacher feedback in final revisions.
- clarity of purpose and awareness of audience.
- organization and development of ideas.
- use of historically accurate information and details.
- attention to spelling, punctuation, grammar, and presentation.

Problem-Solving Groupwork

Problem-Solving Groupwork activities have students working in teams to solve a problem or to complete a task. In evaluating these activities, *process* (how well students work as a team) should be weighed as much as *product* (what the group produces). This can be done by basing half of a student's grade on his or her individual contribution and half on the group's performance or product. These judgments should be based on

- your own observations of the student's ability to work effectively and cooperatively with the group.
- the student's self-assessment of his or her own contributions to the group effort.
- the overall effectiveness of the group's project or performance.

"My teacher gives me and my group a grade when we finish a group project. I think that's the fairest way to grade groupwork."
Middle School Student

Culminating Projects

Traditionally, units of study have culminated in a paper-and-pencil test or unit exam. Such tests are kept secret until the last minute, presumably so that students cannot cheat by studying only what will be covered. Underlying this form of culminating activity is the assumption that a student's recall of specific facts in a test setting is a valid indication that real learning

History Alive!

has taken place. That assumption, however, is based on a narrow view of learning and achievement. As Grant Wiggins has observed, "what is so harmful about current teaching and testing is that they frequently reinforce—unwittingly—the lesson that mere right answers, put forth by going through the motions, are adequate signs of ability."[6]

While the traditional unit test can be used in multiple-ability assessment, it should be only one of many types of culminating activities. Students should also be challenged to demonstrate what they know and can do in a variety of culminating projects. For example, a culminating project might be to write a newspaper representing the South just before the Civil War. Another might be to organize a panel discussion on the question of whether World War I was a "good" war. While the form and scope of such activity-based "exams" are limited only by your imagination and classroom resources, good culminating projects share many or all of the following characteristics:

■ **The project is central to the unit.** It focuses on the key questions, difficult issues, essential understandings, and important concepts of the unit.

■ **The project is known to students in advance.** This kind of exam is not a last-minute creation hidden until test day. Students know at the beginning of a unit how they will be assessed and have time to prepare accordingly.

■ **The project requires students to think deeply about important course content.** Unlike traditional tests with their emphasis on recall, culminating projects challenge students to exercise higher-level thinking skills—comprehension, application, analysis, evaluation, and most important, synthesis—to complete complex problem-solving tasks.

■ **Students are asked to create a meaningful product or performance.** Rather than memorizing content for the final exam, students are encouraged to make use of what they have learned to create a unique product or performance. Instead of answering questions about Lenin's significance, for example, they might create a visual metaphor that represents his place in history.

■ **The project is flexible enough to accommodate different abilities and learning styles.** Well-designed projects tap into more than one kind of intelligence. Many also combine both group and individual activities.

■ **Students know the standards by which their work will be judged.** Standards of excellence are communicated to students when they begin their projects. As they work, students are encouraged to assess their own efforts and to seek feedback from peers or their teacher to use in revising and improving their final product or performance.

■ **The teacher acts as a coach.** When teachers replace tests with projects, their role shifts from that of proctor to coach. Just as a basketball coach does everything within reason to help players perform at their peak on the court, the teacher does everything possible to help students reach the highest level of performance they are capable of on their final projects.

"Culminating projects help me to pull everything together in the end. I get to see how much I've learned."
High School Student

"Culminating projects allow the students to articulate what they learned through learning styles they are comfortable with. I've seen students produce work that I didn't know they were capable of. These projects also lowered students' test-anxiety because they don't have to show everything they know in fifty minutes."
Roger Stock,
High School Teacher

Chapter 9

Three Outstanding Culminating Projects

If like most teachers you were raised in a testing culture, you may find the process of designing and using projects as final exams unusual at first. To help you get started in this alternative form of assessment, here are detailed descriptions of three culminating projects: a visual metaphor project, an oral history project, and a museum project.

☐ A Visual Metaphor Project

Visual metaphor projects challenge students to create metaphorical interpretations of a historical issue, event, or era in a creative and memorable way. Students begin by thinking of an appropriate metaphor in response to a prompt such as, "Stalin was like a _____ ." They draw their metaphor on a large sheet of paper, leaving space for the addition of supporting historical details. A visual metaphor showing Stalin as a bulldozer, for example, might be embellished with such identifying details as his characteristic hat and mustache. To this might be added images of historical events that support this interpretation of the Soviet leader. The final product also includes text, such as a catchy title, supporting historical details, explanations, metaphorical comparisons, and position statements on key issues.

Visual metaphor projects can be used with almost any subject. Below are several ideas to stimulate your thinking, followed by an example of a visual metaphor project that focuses on British Colonialism in India. (For this purpose, make no distinction between a metaphor and a simile, since both involve metaphorical thinking.)

- As the leader of the new Soviet Union, Lenin was like a _____ .
- Marx saw capitalism as _____ , whereas Adam Smith saw it as _____ .
- If Jefferson was a _____ , Hamilton was a _____ .
- The European colonization of Africa was like a _____ .
- Create a metaphor that compares China's road to democracy to that of the Soviet Union.

Preparing Your Students for Visual Metaphor Projects

The first time through any activity is generally anxiety producing for students. This may be particularly true for something as unfamiliar as a visual metaphor project. The following suggestions will help you guide students through the difficult start-up phase:

- Introduce metaphorical thinking to your class weeks before you assign the project. Explain what a metaphor is, show examples from readings, and engage students in elementary metaphorical exercises.
- When you introduce the project, take great care in going over each part of the assignment.
- Draw a rough sketch on the board of what the final project might look like.

These students created a visual metaphor comparing the 1920s to the 1930s.

"The unit's final project allowed me to show what I do know about history, not what I don't know."
High School Student

Unit: **British Colonization of India**
Project Focus: **Should the British be praised for their colonial efforts in India?**

Visual Metaphor Project

Your culminating project, which you may do individually or in pairs, will be to create a visual metaphor that represents the relationship between Great Britain and India during four stages of their history. For each stage you will create a visual based on your metaphor and include factual evidence to support your point of view. Your choice of metaphor should indicate your final stand on this issue: "Should the British be praised for their colonial efforts in India?"

Directions and Requirements

1. Choose one of these metaphors. If you want to use a metaphor not listed here, clear it with your teacher.
   The relationship between Great Britain and India was like the relationship between a boss and the workers; a teacher and students; a parent and children; a coach and the team.

2. Your project should show how this metaphorical relationship worked during four different periods of Indian history.
   - India under control of the Dutch East India Company (1600 to 1858)
   - India as a British colony (1858 through the early 1900s)
   - India fighting for independence (roughly 1915 to 1948)
   - India after independence (1948 to the present)

3. Divide your paper into four panels or sections, one for each period. For each panel, create a visual that shows how your metaphor captures the nature of the relationship between Britain and India during that period. Use drawings, cutouts, photographs, and photocopies to tie your metaphor to events of that period.

4. Write a short explanation for each of your visuals, using evidence and historical details from the period to support your interpretation.

5. Write a *short* paragraph below each visual stating whether or not Britain should be praised for its actions in India during this period and why.

6. Give your completed project a bold title. Your title will probably include references to Britain, India, and your particular metaphor.

Evaluation

Your final product will be judged on
- how well you interpreted your metaphor visually for each period
- how well you supported your interpretations with historical evidence
- the quality of your visual presentation
- the overall creativity of your work
- completion of project requirements

- If your students have done other visual projects, use some of the more successful pieces to model desirable features such as a bold title, a creative border, neat printing, and well-conveyed ideas.
- In the early stages of the project provide additional "scaffolding," information designed to help students focus their thinking on the task at hand.

Evaluating Visual Metaphor Projects

To evaluate visual metaphor projects, some teachers may simply want to make written comments on the back of the completed project. Such comments should reflect the evaluation standards of the original assignment. Another approach is to use an evaluation checklist like the one on page 170. Checklists are relatively easy to use and can be adapted for use as self-assessment and peer-assessment tools. If you use checklists, you may want to give a copy to students along with their assignment. The more explicit your evaluation standards, the higher the quality of projects you will receive.

☐ An Oral History Project

Oral history projects take learning out the classroom and into the community. Students assume the role of historian as they conduct research on a specific topic. Many topics from recent history work well for oral history projects. Among the subjects your students can research are the Great Depression, World War II, the civil-rights movement, the Vietnam War, and immigration.

Once a topic has been selected and refined, students conduct research by interviewing people who lived through and remember the period and events of interest to them. After their interviews, students write up oral history reports, which are then published as part of a class oral history book. The project described in detail below focuses on World War II.

Preparing Your Students for Oral History Projects

Many of your students will not have had any experience in conducting formal interviews. While they may have had many conversations with older people, such as grandparents or neighbors, even the boldest of students may be unnerved by the challenge of interviewing a stranger about the remote past. For the shy or timid student, the prospect can be outright terrifying. Advance preparation is essential to help students get past their fears and to enable them to embark with confidence. One way to prepare them is to model both an effective and an ineffective interview style. Another way is to discuss the do's and don'ts of effective interviewing. The discussion might include the following points:

- Begin with simple background questions that will put the other person at ease.
- Be patient and give the interviewee plenty of time to respond.
- Maintain eye contact.
- Nod your head or say "yes" or "uh-huh" during answers to encourage the interviewee to keep speaking.

This student is conducting an oral interview of a person affected by the Vietnam War.

Unit: British Colonization of India
Project Focus: Should the British be praised for their colonial efforts in India?

Visual Metaphor Project: Evaluation Checklist

Name _____

	Needs work	Good	Outstanding
1. Metaphorical Interpretation			
■ The central metaphor is clear and easily understood.	____	____	____
■ Visual details support, explain, and extend the central metaphor.	____	____	____
2. Historical Evidence			
■ Adequate evidence is provided to support the central metaphor convincingly.	____	____	____
■ Supporting historical details are stated clearly and accurately.	____	____	____
3. Visual Presentation			
■ Visual elements are laid out in an interesting and colorful way.	____	____	____
■ Text is neat and legible.	____	____	____
4. Overall Creativity			
■ Striking, inventive, or amusing visual images used.	____	____	____
■ Language is interesting and colorful.	____	____	____
5. Project Requirements			
■ Four metaphorical drawings are included.	____	____	____
■ These written elements are included: (1) title, (2) historical explanations for each period, (3) stand on the unit question for each period.	____	____	____

Comments

- As you ask questions, lean forward to indicate interest. Slouching tells the interviewee that you aren't interested in what is being said.
- Ask open-ended rather than simple "yes" or "no" questions. Instead of asking "Were you scared?" try asking, "How did you feel?"
- Don't interrupt the interviewee during an answer.
- Be polite at all times.

Evaluating Oral History Projects

Once students have completed the first drafts of their reports, you might have them work in pairs or small groups to read and evaluate their own and each other's work using an evaluation checklist like the one on page 174. Encourage students to incorporate this feedback into their final drafts.

☐ A Museum Project

In a museum project, students work in groups to create exhibits that represent the accomplishments and legacies of a historical era, culture, or social or political movement. Museum exhibits are designed on tag board, construction paper, or butcher paper using a variety of devices—pictures, replications of art and artifacts, historical summaries, primary source documents, graphic displays, maps—to capture the essence and significance of the topic. Groups incorporate both materials that they accumulated throughout a unit—original writing, visuals, historical quotes—and resources that they collect through research. In addition, groups are challenged to arrange their exhibit artfully and professionally.

Museum projects are appropriate for almost any historical subject, since many museums function expressly to commemorate the past. On page 175 are guidelines students might receive for a museum project at the end of a unit on the rise of Islam.

"We must constantly remind ourselves that the ultimate purpose of evaluation is to enable students to evaluate themselves. Educators may have been practicing this skill to the exclusion of learners; we need to shift part of that responsibility to students. Fostering students' ability to direct and redirect themselves must be a major goal—or what is education for?"[7]

Arthur Costa

Unit: World War II
Project Focus: Are Americans justified in looking back on World War II as the "last good war"?

Oral History Project

For this culminating project, you will conduct an oral history interview of someone who lived through World War II. Your interview subject might be an individual who served in the armed forces or a civilian with memories of wartime life on the home front. After completing your interview, you will write up that person's story as if you were a historian. Your final effort will be published as part of our class oral history collection.

Directions and Requirements

1. Identify someone who is old enough to remember World War II, and make arrangements to conduct an oral history interview. Your interview should focus on one of the following six topics. If you want to use a topic not listed here, clear it with your teacher.

    - The events leading up to the war
    - The attack on Pearl Harbor
    - Life on the home front
    - Life in the armed forces
    - The Holocaust
    - Dropping the atomic bomb

2. When you conduct your interview, keep the following suggestions in mind.

    - Introduce yourself if necessary, and then explain what this project is about.
    - If you plan to use a tape recorder, be sure to get permission to record before you start. Otherwise, plan to take good notes.
    - Open the interview with a few warm-up questions such as: How old were you during World War II? Where did you live? Were you in the armed forces? If so, which branch? If not, what did you do during the war? This information will help you to decide which of the six topics above to focus on in your interview.
    - Use follow-up questions to draw out interesting stories and details.
    - Be aware that some people may not want to discuss painful subjects in depth. Be sensitive and considerate.
    - At the end of the interview, explain that you will write up what you have learned and that this story will become part of your class's oral history collection. Find out whether your subject would like to be referred to by name or would prefer to remain anonymous in this sharing process.

Oral History Project page 2

3. Use your interview notes or recording to write a short oral history. About half of this history should be written in your own words, with the other half made up of direct quotations (from the person you interviewed). Try to write this person's history so it will be interesting to the reader. For example, if there is a dramatic moment, you might want to keep it for the end of the story.

4. Prepare a final copy of your oral history for publication following these guidelines:
   - Your final piece should be three to five pages long.
   - Give your piece a catchy title.
   - Include a short biographical paragraph at the end of your history explaining the background of the person you interviewed.
   - Put your name on your finished piece, either below the title or at the end.
   - Type or put on a computer your oral history if at all possible. If not, print your final draft neatly.
   - Include a visual with your history. It might be a drawing, a graphic design, a photograph, or a photocopy of a picture from your text.

Evaluation

Your oral history will be judged on
- how well you hold the reader's interest
- your use of quotations to support your story
- attention to writing mechanics
- visual presentation
- completion of project requirements

Unit: World War II
Project Focus: Are Americans justified in looking back on World War II as the "last good war"?

Oral History Project: Evaluation Checklist

Name _____

	Needs work	Good	Outstanding

1. Writing Style

- The writing is colorful, lively, and holds the reader's interest. ____ ____ ____
- The story is well-organized, with a beginning, middle, and end. ____ ____ ____

2. Use of Interview Results

- Quotations are used to support the main points of the story. ____ ____ ____
- The reader hears the interviewee's voice as clearly as the author's voice. ____ ____ ____

3. Writing Mechanics

- Words are correctly spelled and capitalized. ____ ____ ____
- Sentences and quotations are punctuated properly. ____ ____ ____

4. Visual Presentation

- The story is typed, word-processed, or neatly printed. ____ ____ ____
- The story includes an appropriate visual to accompany the text. ____ ____ ____

5. Project Requirements

- The final project includes a title, author line, and biographical paragraph about the interviewee. ____ ____ ____
- The text is three to five pages. ____ ____ ____

Strengths

Areas of Improvement

Unit: **The Rise of Islam**
Project Focus: **How were people's lives affected by the rise of Islam?**

Museum Project

In this unit we examined the rise of Islam and focused on four topics: the roots of Islam, the expansion of Islam, the Golden Age of Islam, and the Crusades. For your culminating project, you will work in groups to create a museum with four exhibits. Each exhibit will represent one of the four topics we studied and should be designed to educate museumgoers on the most important ideas of the topic.

Directions and Requirements

1. Your project should focus on how people's lives were affected by the rise of Islam. It should be comprised of four exhibits, each of which will address one of these historical topics in the rise of Islam:

   - The roots of Islam
   - The expansion of Islam
   - The Golden Age of Islam
   - The Crusades

2. Each exhibit should combine two to four of the following devices to (1) represent the important ideas of the period and (2) address the project focus question:

   - Pictures
   - Dioramas
   - Metaphorical symbols
   - Music
   - Charts and tables
   - Captions
   - Time lines
   - Collages
   - Annotated maps
   - Replications of art and artifacts
   - Quotes
   - Replications of primary source documents
   - Audio-visual displays
   - Computer-generated displays

3. Each exhibit must have a written plaque that introduces museumgoers to the importance of the period represented in the exhibit. Each should be one to two paragraphs in length. Place these plaques at the "entrance" of each exhibit.

4. Your group must decide how to arrange the project in a logical, artful way by creating a blueprint to help plan the use of space for each exhibit.

5. Each member of your group will be responsible for brainstorming ideas, researching and contributing information, designing the exhibits, and acting as docent (a trained guide). In addition, each student will be assigned one of the following roles:

Museum Project page 2

Curator: Lists all topics to be included in each exhibit. Plans the use of space for each exhibit. Coordinates the production of the project.

Historical Writer: Writes the text for the four plaques.

Graphic Artist: Designs all graphic elements—illustrations, maps, collages—for each exhibit.

Contractor: Glues and assembles all parts of each exhibit.

Evaluation

Your final project will be judged on
- how well the exhibits answer the topic question
- the visual appeal of the exhibits
- how thoroughly the exhibits cover the important ideas of the four topic areas
- the accuracy of the introduction for each exhibit
- consistent and purposeful groupwork
- the use of cooperative skills to complete the project

Unit: The Rise of Islam
Project Focus: How were people's lives affected by the rise of Islam?

Museum Project: Evaluation Checklist

Name _____

	Needs work	Good	Outstanding

1. Quality of Museum Exhibits
   - Exhibits focused on the most important historical topics.   ____ ____ ____
   - Exhibits answered the project focus question.   ____ ____ ____
   - Plaques are concise and accurate.   ____ ____ ____

2. Visual Appeal of Museum Exhibits
   - Effective use of a wide variety of written and visual devices.   ____ ____ ____
   - Museum was organized and displayed artfully and professionally.   ____ ____ ____

3. Effectiveness of Group Interaction
   - Group members worked consistently and purposefully.   ____ ____ ____
   - Group used cooperative skills to complete the project.   ____ ____ ____

4. Individual Contribution
   - Contributed ideas at all stages of the project.   ____ ____ ____
   - Shared equally in the planning, research, and design responsibilities.   ____ ____ ____
   - Effectively carried out the responsibilities of the role.   ____ ____ ____

Comments

© Addison-Wesley Publishing Company, Inc.

Preparing Your Students

As with visual metaphor projects, first exposure to a project as unfamiliar as a museum is generally anxiety producing. The following suggestions will help you guide students through the difficult start-up phase.

- Introduce students to the purpose and function of museums. Discuss different ways museums create displays that are interesting and educational.
- When you introduce the project, take care in going over each part of the assignment.
- Draw a rough sketch on the board of what the final project might look like.
- If your students have done other museum projects, use some of the more successful products to model desirable features such as interesting design, use of a variety of displays, concise writing, and creative display.
- Emphasize the importance of following a step-by-step plan to conceive of and complete the museum.

Evaluating Museum Projects

Museum projects, like any culminating project that requires groupwork, must be evaluated for both individual and group contributions. Place equal grading weight on these two factors: (1) the individual contribution to the group effort and (2) the overall quality of the final product.

To facilitate the evaluation process, have students complete a groupwork Brag Sheet (see p. 87). This, coupled with your own observations, will help you determine relative contribution of each student during the project. To formulate a product grade, simply review the museum exhibits in light of the evaluation standards in the student handout. You can record grades on the back of the museum exhibits.

Alternatively, you may want to use an evaluation checklist like the one on p. 177. They are easy to use and can be adapted for use as a self-assessment tool.

Notes and Credits

Reading Notes

Introduction

[1] Diane Ravitch and Chester Finn, Jr., *What Do Our 17-Year-Olds Know? A Report on the First National Assessment of History and Literature* (New York: Harper and Row, 1987). [2] James A. Banks, *Multicultural Education: Issues and Perspectives,* Second Edition, (Needham Heights, Mass.: Allyn and Bacon, 1993). [3] Howard Gardner, *Frames of Mind: The Theory of Multiple Intelligences* (New York: Basic Books, Inc., 1983). [4] Anne Wheelock, *Crossing the Tracks: How "Untracking" Can Save America's Schools* (New York: The New Press, 1992), p. 91. [5] Gardner, *Frames of Mind.* [6] Danielle Lapp, "(Nearly) Total Recall," *The Stanford Magazine,* Dec. 1992, pp. 48–49. [7] Gardner, *Frames of Mind,* p. 38. [8] Elizabeth Cohen, *Designing Groupwork: Strategies for the Heterogeneous Classroom* (New York: Columbia University Teachers College, 1986), p. 6. [9] Ibid. p. 28. [10] Joseph Berger, Susan Rosenholtz, and Morris Zelditch, Jr., "Status Organizing Processes," *Annual Review of Sociology,* Vol. 6 (1980), pp. 479–508. [11] Jerome Bruner, *The Process of Education* (Cambridge, Mass.: Harvard University Press, 1960), p. 33. [12] Fred M. Newmann, Joseph Onosko, and Robert B. Stevenson, "Staff Development for Higher-Order Thinking: A Synthesis of Practical Wisdom," *Journal of Staff Development,* Vol. 11, No. 3, pp. 48–55. [13] Ibid. [14] Benjamin Bloom, *Taxonomy of Educational Objectives* (New York: Longman Inc., 1986).

Chapter 1

[1] Larry Cuban, *How Teachers Taught: Constancy and Change in American Classrooms* (New York: Longman Inc., 1984).

Chapter 4

[1] Cohen, *Designing Groupwork,* pp. 145–155. [2] Ibid. p. 35. [3] Jane Stallings and Deborah Stipek, "Research on Early Childhood and Elementary School Teaching Programs, *Handbook of Research on Teaching,* Third Edition (New York: Macmillan Publishing Company, 1986), p. 750. [4] Gardner, *Frames of Mind.* [5] Howard Gardner, *The Unschooled Mind* (New York: Basic Books, Inc., 1991), p. 13. [6] Cohen, *Designing Groupwork,* p. 115. [7] Lyn Corno and Richard E. Snow, "Adapting Teaching to Individual Differences Among Learners," *Handbook of Research on Teaching,* Third Edition (New York: Macmilliam Publishing Company, 1986), p. 622. [8] Grant Wiggins, *Educational Leadership,* Vol. 49, No. 8, p. 29.

Chapter 5

[1] National Institute of Education, Report of Panel 5: *Teaching As a Linguistic Process in a Cultural Setting,* Conference on studies in teaching (1974), p. 1.

Chapter 6

[1] Bruner, *The Process of Education,* p. 24. [2] Richard E. Young, Alton L. Becker, and Kenneth L. Pike, *Rhetoric: Discovery and Change* (New York: Harcourt Brace, 1970), p. 237. [3] Gary Tate and Edward P. J. Corbett, eds., *The Writing Teacher's Sourcebook* (New York: Oxford University Press, 1981), p. 171. [4] Dan Kirby and Tom Liner, *Inside Out: Developmental Strategies for Teaching Writing* (New Jersey: Boynton/Cook Publishers, Inc., 1981), p. 46. [5] Ibid. [6] Jerome Bruner, *On Knowing: Essays for the Left Hand* (New York: Athenaeum, 1965).

Notes and Credits

Chapter 7

[1]Robert Hughes, "The Fraying of America," *Time,* Feb. 3, 1992, p. 47. [2]Survey conducted by John Hopkins University, 1984. [3]Gardner, *Frames of Mind.* [4]Cohen, *Designing Groupwork,* p. 6. [5]Bruner, *The Process of Education,* p. 33.

Chapter 9

[1]Dale Carlson, "Changing the Face of Testing in California," *California Curriculum News Report,* Jan.-Feb. 1991, p. 1. [2]Pat Nickell, "Doing the Stuff of Social Studies: A Conversation with Grant Wiggins," *Social Education,* Vol. 56, No. 2 (Feb. 1992), p. 92.[3]Grant Wiggins, "A True Test: Toward More Authentic and Equitable Assessment," *Phi Delta Kappan,* May 1989, p. 710. [4]Vito Perrone, *Expanding Student Assessment* (Alexandria, Va.: Association for Supervision and Curriculum Development, 1991), p. 37. [5]Nickell, "Doing the Stuff of Social Studies," p. 94. [6]Wiggins, "A True Test," p. 706. [7]Benjamin Bloom, "The Search for Methods of Group Instruction as Effective as One-on-one Tutoring," *Educational Leadership,* May 1984, p. 14. [8]Arthur Costa and Robert J. Marzano, "Question: Do Standardized Test Measure General Cognitive Skills? Answer: No," *Educational Leadership,* Vol. 45, No. 8 (May 1988), pp. 66–71.

Credits

p. 17: Library of Congress.

Introduction

p. 24, bottom: Library of Congress; p. 28: U.S. Army Historical Collection; p. 29: U.S. Army Historical Collection; p. 30: U.S. Army Historical Collection; p. 31: Library of Congress; p. 32: Library of Congress; p. 34, bottom: U.S. Army Historical Collection; p. 36, bottom: Library of Congress; p. 38: National Archives; p. 39: Library of Congress.

Chapter 1

p. 52: Library of Congress; p. 53: Arizona Historical Society Library, Roskruge Collection; p. 54: Library of Congress.

Chapter 2

p. 77: Library of Congress; p. 79: Library of Congress; p. 89, top: U.S. Army Historical Collection.

Chapter 4

p. 98: Library of Congress; p. 99: Cinema Center Films; p. 104: Library of Congress; p. 105: The Bettman Archive, courtesy Tom Gleeson, St. Anthony Foundation.

Chapter 5

p. 109: Library of Congress; p. 111: Library of Congress; p. 116: Smithsonian Institution.

Chapter 6

Cover photograph and photographs on pages 1, 21, and 125: Library of Congress; U.S. Army Historical Collection; Kingmond Young. All other photographs by Kingmond Young.

History Alive! Materials

When you look into a teaching unit from Teachers' Curriculum Institute, you'll find all the ideas and resources you need to make the History Alive! approach work for you.

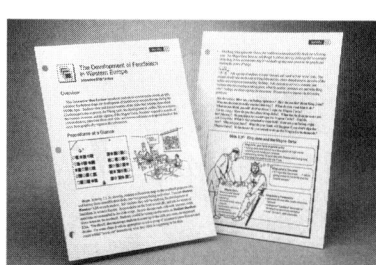

Each unit comes with logically sequenced lesson plans written by teachers. Use as presented or supplement with your own ideas and creativity.

Student handouts include clear visuals and an easy-to-use format that is highly effective for students with diverse learning styles.

Each unit includes slides and overhead transparencies to make your teaching visual and interactive. Middle school units come with historical music.

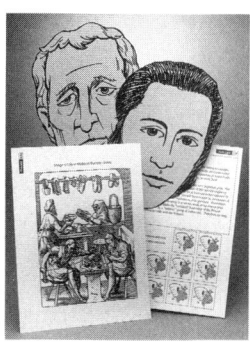

Every program has a wealth of hands-on materials—historical masks, plastic-covered placards with rich primary-source documents, biographies for simulations, art reproductions, literary excerpts, and more—to make learning memorable.

Middle School World History Program

Unit 1 **Europe After the Fall of the Roman Empire**
- The Fall of the Roman Empire
- The Rise of the Byzantine Empire
- The Development of Feudalism in Europe
- The Church's Power in Medieval Europe

Unit 2 **The Rise of Islam**
- The Revelation of Islam
- The Development of an Islamic Civilization
- The Golden Age of Muslims
- The Crusades

Unit 3 **Empires and Kingdoms in Sub-Saharan Africa**
- Understanding the Geography of Sub-Saharan Africa
- Empires of West Africa: Ghana, Mali, and Songhay
- Kingdoms of Central and Southern Africa
- African Traditions: From Past to Present

Unit 4 **Imperial China and Feudal Japan**
- A Thousand Years of Dynastic Rule in China
- The Flowering of Chinese Culture
- The Development of Feudalism in Japan
- Culture in the Land of the Rising Sun

Unit 5 **Europe's Transition to the Modern World**
- The Renaissance
- The Reformation
- The Age of Exploration

Unit 6 **Civilizations of the Americas**
- The Geography of Latin America
- The Maya
- The Inca
- The Aztecs
- Two Visions of the Spanish Conquest

Middle School U.S. History Program

Unit 1 Geography of America from Past to Present
- Reviewing Basic Geography
- Learning the Physiographic Features of the United States
- Adapting to the Environment: Native Americans
- Adapting to the Environment: Colonial Settlers

Unit 2 Colonial Life and the American Revolution
- Examining Colonial Society
- Slavery in the Colonies
- Growing Conflict with England
- Toward Independence

Unit 3 The Constitution in a New Nation
- The Roots of Government
- The Creation of the Constitution
- The Creation of the Bill of Rights
- The Constitution in Action, 1789–1820
- The Constitution in Action Today

Unit 4 Manifest Destiny in a Growing Nation
- America Discovers Its Manifest Destiny
- The Heritage of the Southwest
- Many Paths to the West
- Through the Eyes of Native Americans
- A Case Study of Reform: Women's Rights

Unit 5 The Civil War and Reconstruction
- Contrasting North and South
- The Coming of the Civil War
- A Family Divided: Fighting the Civil War
- Reconstructing the Union

Unit 6 The Rise of Industrial America
- Industrializing America
- Immigration: The Changing Face of America
- The Progressive Response

High School Twentieth Century U.S. History Program

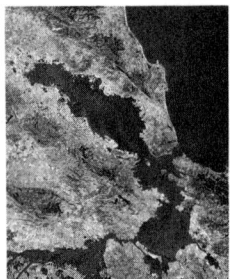

Unit 1 **Mapping the United States**
- Reviewing Basic Geography
- Learning the Physiographic Features of the United States
- Settling the Land

Unit 2 **The Progressive Era**
- The Immigrants
- The Industrialists
- The Progressives

Unit 3 **The United States Emerges as a World Power**
- Growth of Imperialism
- Woodrow Wilson and World War I
- The End of World War I and Its Legacy

Unit 4 **The Roaring Twenties**
- Postwar Tensions
- Republicans in Command
- Life in the 1920s

Unit 5 **The Great Depression and the New Deal**
- The Coming of the Depression
- The Human Impact of the Depression
- The New Deal
- The Legacy of the New Deal

Unit 6 **World War II**
- Coming of the War
- The Holocaust
- The United States Goes to War
- The War Front and the Atomic Bomb

Unit 7 **The Cold War**
- Ideological Origins of the Cold War
- Early Cold War Tensions
- The Cold War Gets Hot: A Case Study of Vietnam
- The Legacy of the Cold War

Unit 8 **The Civil Rights Movement**
- From Enslavement to Jim Crow
- The Struggle for Equal Rights
- Civil Rights Today

Unit 9 **American Society in the 50s and 60s**
- The 1950s: Pursuing the American Dream
- The Early 1960s: Kennedy's Youthful Idealism
- Idealism Dashed: Social Upheaval
- Case Study: Does Media Shape Our Perception of Women?

Professional Development Programs

TCI conducts a wide range of professional development programs:

- **One-Day On-Site Workshops** In these district and school-site sponsored trainings, the workshop leader demonstrates TCI's six powerful teaching strategies for diverse learners and shows how to apply the theories of multiple intelligences and cooperative interaction to the social studies classroom.

- **Two-Day On-Site Workshops** In these district and school-site sponsored trainings, the workshop leader covers the same topics as the one-day workshop as well as (1) creating a cooperative, tolerant classroom, (2) using interactive student notebooks, (3) multiple-ability assessment strategies, and (4) using a thematic approach to history teaching.

- **Summer Institutes** In these one-week summer institutes, TCI works with teachers in specific content areas to help them design their own dynamic curriculum along the TCI model. Institutes focus on subjects such as World History, U.S. History, and social studies instruction for limited-English-proficient students.

- **Seminar Series** TCI sponsors a series of regional, one-day workshops designed to introduce teachers to the TCI approach. Dates and locations for these seminars are announced in special mailings you can receive by calling TCI.

- **TCI Conferences** TCI sponsors its annual two-day conference as a forum for teachers to discuss their experiences with TCI strategies and curriculum. Dates and locations are announced in special mailings you can receive by calling TCI.

- **On-Going Consultation** TCI offers a variety of additional professional development activities including advanced workshops, follow-up work with teachers, model teaching by TCI teachers in your classrooms, and support in curriculum development.

To schedule a workshop for your site or to obtain a calendar of upcoming events, please call 1-800-497-6138.

Order Form

Mail to: TCI, 201 San Antonio Circle, Ste. 105, Mountain View CA 94040 Fax: 415-948-9303 Or call: 1-800-497-6138

Bill to
Name _____
Organization _____
Address _____
City _____
State _____ Zip _____

Ship to
Name _____
Organization _____
Address _____
City _____
State _____ Zip _____

Method of Payment
☐ Check # _____ ☐ Purchase Order # _____
☐ VISA _____ ☐ MasterCard _____

Card Number _____ Expiration Date _____
Signature _____ Telephone _____

Please note: Discounts are already calculated into the price of the entire program. Returns receive full cash or credit, less a 15% restocking charge, if in good condition. Units shipped 3 to 4 weeks after receipt of order.

Order No.		Qty.	Price	Total
TCI-002	*History Alive!*		$23.⁹⁶	
WH-07-0	**Middle School World History Program**		$2,000.⁰⁰	
WH-07-1	Europe After the Fall of the Roman Empire		350.⁰⁰	
WH-07-2	The Rise of Islam		350.⁰⁰	
WH-07-3	Empires and Kingdoms of Sub-Saharan Africa		350.⁰⁰	
WH-07-4	Imperial China and Feudal Japan		350.⁰⁰	
WH-07-5	Europe's Transition to the Modern World		350.⁰⁰	
WH-07-6	Civilizations of the Americas		350.⁰⁰	
USH-08-0	**Middle School U.S. History Program**		$2,000.⁰⁰	
USH-08-1	Geography of America from Past to Present		350.⁰⁰	
USH-08-2	Colonial Life and the American Revolution		350.⁰⁰	
USH-08-3	The Constitution in a New Nation		350.⁰⁰	
USH-08-4	Manifest Destiny in a Growing Nation		350.⁰⁰	
USH-08-5	The Civil War and Reconstruction		350.⁰⁰	
USH-08-6	The Rise of Industrial America		350.⁰⁰	
USH-11-0	**High School 20th Century U.S. History Program**		$2,000.⁰⁰	
USH-11-1	Mapping the United States		250.⁰⁰	
USH-11-2	The Progressive Era		250.⁰⁰	
USH-11-3	The United States Emerges as a World Power		250.⁰⁰	
USH-11-4	The Roaring Twenties		250.⁰⁰	
USH-11-5	The Great Depression and the New Deal		250.⁰⁰	
USH-11-6	World War II		250.⁰⁰	
USH-11-7	The Cold War		250.⁰⁰	
USH-11-8	The Civil Rights Movement		250.⁰⁰	
USH-11-9	American Society in the 50s and 60s		250.⁰⁰	
			Subtotal	
			Applicable Sales Tax	
			3% Shipping	
			Total	